THANK YOU VERY MUCH!

Copyright 2020, Rick Vuyst, All Rights Reserved

No part of this book may be reproduced, stored in a retrieval system, or transmitted by any means without the written permission of the author.

ISBN 978-1-61808-197-1

Printed in the United States of America

Scripture quotations marked (NIV) are taken from the Holy Bible, New International Version®, NIV®. Copyright © 1973, 1978, 1984, 2011 by Biblica, Inc.™ Used by permission of Zondervan. All rights reserved worldwide. www.zondervan.com. The "NIV" and "New International Version" are trademarks registered in the United States Patent and Trademark Office by Biblica, Inc.™

I Need to Change My Plants

Rick Vuyst

Table of Contents

Foreword – An Ode to Plants in Times of Trouble
Chapter One – Necessity the Mother of Invention
   The "Jean" Pool 1
Chapter Two – Bramble On 7
Chapter Three – 2020 Vision 21
Chapter Four – My Fra Mauro Formation 37
Chapter Five – Oakley Oracles 53
Chapter Six – Between a Grok and a Hard Place 71
Chapter Seven – Quintessential Normalcy 87
Chapter Eight – Tactical Dispersal 107
Chapter Nine – Get Busy Lizzy 117
Chapter Ten – It's Good for What "Ales" You 125
Chapter Eleven – Improve Your Plot in Life 137
Chapter Twelve – Teasel and the Dame's Rockets 151
Chapter Thirteen – They Don't Even Know I Xyst 165
Chapter Fourteen – Plantasm 179
Chapter Fifteen – Under House Arrest 189
Chapter Sixteen – A Joule in My Crown 201
Chapter Seventeen – The Kale of the Wild 211
Chapter Eighteen – I Need to Change My Plants 223
Chapter Nineteen – Under the Vine and Fig 241
Chapter Twenty – Owl be Home for Christmas 255

Dedication

This book is dedicated to those who inspired me at a young age to love history and stories. I have learned that assessing past examples of change is vital to understanding change in an ever-changing world. Stories well done reveal how people and societies have reacted to a crisis or adapted. Change is hard. Forced change is harder. People live in the present but are forever and always planning and worrying about the future. History offers a storehouse of information about how people and societies behave in the present. It is an evidential base for projection of what is to come. The past contributed to the present, and therefore also the future. Change is inevitable so developing a capacity for determining the magnitude and significance of change, in other words maintaining perspective, provides a solid grasp of the human experience. History teaches by example like the influential "Oakleys" in life who don't tell you how to do it ... they show you how.

Foreword

An Ode to Plants in Times of Trouble

I shut off the lawnmower and dropped to my knees on the lawn. I feel the damp cooling of the turf on my stained knees as I bend over to get a closer look. My neighbors probably thought I had overheated. Actually my curiosity got the best of me. Taking a closer look, and, based on my best estimates and calculations, I determined that there were 27 grass blades to a typical square inch of lawn. With 144 square inches to a square foot, I multiplied 27 blades times 144 to determine I had 3,888 blades of grass in every square foot of my lawn. Staggering to think if the typical small home lawn in the suburbs is 5,000 square feet that there are 19,940,000 blades of grass in that lawn. And if you don't believe me you count them yourself.

The struggle for the crown always makes a good plot

Grass roots and shoots meet at the crown. The crown is the swollen light colored part of the grass plant located at soil level. It is the headquarters or control center for the grass plants, because it contains many nodes, each with an attached bud that could produce a new, independent plant, called a tiller. The crown is the king of turf growth. "Lawn" live the king. Because the crown is at soil level, it escapes cutting and continues to support regrowth for trimmed blades and generate new tillers. That is, however, if the lawn is not scalped or cut too short, putting stress on the crown and providing an opening for weed proliferation. Raising the deck on the mower shades the crown and gives the turf a competitive advantage over the survivalist weeds.

Lawns are a way of taming nature in an age when urban dwellers live in developments and cut trees down naming the streets after them. On Elm street lawns are a means homeowners use to map their sociographic plot or territory.

Within my plot the drone of the mower, or maybe the exhaust, had caused my mind to wander and speculate. I thought with such an impressive vegetative population of over 19 million blades why is it the **weeds get all the attention?** If the weeds account for only one or two percent of the density, why do they tend to be the focus?

Negative things get our attention.

We've heard the old pithy proverbs:

The nail that stands out gets pounded down.
The large tree catches more wind.
The squeaky wheelbarrow wheel gets the oil.

Why does it seem negative thoughts want more attention and we dwell on them longer? They take more space in our heads if we let them. It's like renting out space in your head for free. We chew on them longer than positive thoughts. Maybe negativity is easier than being positive? Anyone can tear down a potting shed but not everyone can build one. If we absorb and then dwell on negative stimuli, it will capture our attention and take up the space in our head like weeds. We have to consciously root them out.

2020 was a year we could have easily focused on the weeds, the negative. There were so many weeds it was tough to keep up. Even the basics were a kerfuffle. During the week of March 16, 2020 toilet paper became scarce with sales rising 845% compared to the month prior, and suddenly bathroom tissue was a number one seller. Not euphemistically number two anymore, it was in high demand and store shelves cleared. There is precedent in history for such activity, and, as the famous Yankee catcher Yogi Berra would say, it's deja vu all over again. If history repeats itself, toilet paper was the classic example as I will explain in this book.

If you look to the past (study history) there are answers for how to react in the present.

After stay-at-home orders to deal with a pandemic, I noticed three types emerged from quarantine. "Plumped" (ate too much) "Pumped" (used the time to workout) or "Stumped" (where do we go from here). All three are better than a "grump." Some friends become enemies, some enemies become friends, a person's true character emerges quicker in a crisis than a bean seed germinates in warm soil.

As hoarding, the absurd and frustration ensued, it would be easy to overlook all the good that was happening around us. A refocus. Sowing seeds for good. Community cultivation. Weeds don't have to get all the attention. If we decide what our focus will be... then it will be. In our search to be grounded what I call a "plant-demos" broke out all over. Plants are healing. Indoor plants are "foundational" for home's interiors, as the more uncertainty we feel about the outside world, the more well being we want for our inside world.

Gardening is therapy because it makes you feel better. And when you feel better it spreads to others. It's contagious.

"A Plant-demos"

Greek *pándēmos* of all the people, public, common, widespread + dēmos,"district, country, people"

mid 17th century: from Greek *pandēmos* (from pan 'all' + dēmos 'people') + -ic

It's not the first time in history that during times of crisis we experienced a "plant-demos" with plants, soil, growth, renewal, and a return to the garden for **all** people. It has been that way since the Garden of Eden itself; a place of peace and bounty, then judgment, and finally a promise of restoration. The basis for my **"plant-demos"** play on words is the **root** origin of the word pandemic. The word pandemic comes from the Latin word *pandemus*, which itself comes from the Greek *pandemos*, *pan* meaning "all, every, whole" and *dēmos*, meaning "people" or **all** the people. "Demos" are the common people, the populace in a democracy. It is evident that plants are fundamental, of intrinsic value and for **ALL** the people. In biology "deme" is a local population of organisms of the same kind, especially one in which the genetic mix is similar throughout the group. In other words we are in this together. In any crisis we instinctively search our roots, longing for the comfort of activities that ground us. **A gardening renaissance**. Interaction with plants is a constitutive act. It is part of our personal constitution. Look up synonyms for constitution. You will see words like vitality, essence, formation, character. Top of the list in my search for words relating to our constitution? The word **nature**. Yes it's in our nature.

History repeats itself as we were again reminded in 2020. If we had a crystal ball we wouldn't have to be as quick on our feet. But we have history to look back on. We work our way through experimenting as we go. It was one of Ben Franklin's friends, Joseph Priestly, who engaged in experimentation for the general well-being of his fellow man. In the course of these experiments, Joseph Priestley made a significant and meaningful observation. A flame would go out when placed in a jar, and the resident mouse would die. Both the flame and the rodent failed due to lack of air. Putting a green plant in the jar and exposing it to sunlight would "refresh" the air, permitting a flame to burn and the mouse to breathe. Priestley wrote, "the injury which is continually done to the mouse is in part at least, repaired by the vegetable creation."

He had observed that plants release oxygen into the air, and he hypothesized on the process known to us as photosynthesis. You could say the end results were a validation of the importance of plants and that in his experimentation Priestly needed to change his plants, resulting in mouse to mouse resuscitation.

This is a book of stories, historical precedent and how gardening came to the rescue one year. I love plants, history and health. As a 60 year old man I also am not immune to the rapid rate of change. I can't put my head in the sand and pretend it isn't happening. I call it 2020 vision.

The Garden invites us to live in liminal space. We find liminal space by putting our hands in the dirt.

The word liminal comes from the Latin word '*limen*', meaning threshold. Any point or place of entering or beginning. A liminal space is the time between the past and what is coming next. Not living in the past and not knowing what the future will bring, in other words it's not settled yet. It's planting, it's cultivating not knowing what comes next. It's weird, yet beautiful, an in between space. It is a place of transition, a season of waiting, and not knowing. A place to plant seeds. We discover beauty sometimes in the most unexpected places, because that's where God hides His greatest treasures. And what could be more marginalized than dirt? Yet it's the foundation of many beautiful things. The aroma of soil in spring when the winter is past is a liminal space. And whether it's people or plants I always believe there is more good than is initially seen. Many times it is found at the margins because there is purpose, beauty, great expectations to be found in the margins. The garden is

> Your purpose is often embedded in the pain. It is only natural that spring follows winter.

a great place to celebrate margins. Think of Genesis. It's not land, it's not sky, it's the place in between, a garden. And we are called to cultivate and celebrate it with those around us weeds and all.

Liminal space is where transformation takes place, if we are patient and let it shape us. It's called being grounded. If we don't encounter liminal space in our lives, we start idealizing what we assume to be "normalcy" and trust me no two seasons are the same. When "normal" doesn't happen it upends the status quo. There is a ripple effect. Like the changing soil temperature in spring, unseen to the eye, the ripple effect is an explosion of growth eventually evident to all. It is these transitions that are an invitation to growth. Nature shows us time and again.

After surviving the upheaval of a tumultuous year of weeds I find myself more attuned to reflection not rumination. Rumination is the focused attention on the symptoms of one's distress and on its possible causes and consequences, and not necessarily solutions. I wanted answers and reflected on what I was learning. This is my 2020 vision from a botanically ground level. We as humans like patterns so we can anticipate what's going to happen. That's why we love the seasons. We celebrate them with almost a Pavlovian response. A seasonal cadence. There is a rhythm to life. Seasons. I think we love gardening because it is linear in a world where technological progress is exponential. Technology today progresses so fast that the linear expectations of preparation, plant, nurture and harvest has a comforting effect on our personal state. Progressively predictable.

Today the default response to the question "how are you?" has shifted from "fine" or "good" to "busy," because the pace of change continues to accelerate. The major distinction between linear and exponential functions is the rate of their growth. That's what makes the garden such a great place. The growth is at a pace with seasonally embraced changes. It is true that in a digital and computer age we need more tactile experiences, and gardening provides that lifestyle, a natural progressive experience. I need to change my plants.

As I understand it, to wax means to grow, and, if you wax poetic, you grow philosophical. I've grown all manner of vegetation in my life, but will my 2020 experience cause me to grow philosophical? I know I can be poetic. I am fond of limericks and formulate them in my head while dealing with conundrums. A limerick is a five-line poem that consists of a single stanza, an AABBA rhyme scheme, and whose subject is a short, pithy tale or description. Most limericks are trivial in nature and their formulation a mental distraction or exercise. It's a means of coping. It's because a poet like me can survive anything, even 2020, but not a misspelled word.

An Ode to Plants in Times of Trouble

Resisting the impulse to brood,
Despite trouble I sought gratitude,
I adjusted my mood
And could only conclude
I'm responsible for my attitude.

Sometimes when I feel introspective
I realize my mood is elective
I straighten my course
Good thoughts I endorse
And get busy maintaining perspective

Taking a positive stance
I worked to ignore negative rants
We dug in the dirt
Sad thoughts to subvert
We did it by changing our plants

So to those who are disenchanted
The noise can be somewhat slanted
Seek out your roots
And harvest the fruits
When your feet are firmly planted.

It all seemed so apropos
Things no longer the status quo
Supply and demand
Created a brand
My jeans are indigo

Chapter One
Necessity the Mother of Invention

The "Jean" Pool

IF YOUR FEET ARE ALWAYS FIRMLY planted on the ground, it makes it hard to put your pants on. We all have a smidgen of rebel in us ... maybe even a small unseen unexpressed side of recalcitrant behavior in our genes. Jeans were the preferred clothing of cowboys and west-coast miners for decades, but in the 1950s they became the apparel of a restless edgy freewheeling hero: the rebel on a motorcycle. Not that I was looking to be an iconoclastic rabble rouser; they did symbolize freedom even though I didn't own a motorcycle.

Jeans were an independent personal statement even though ***everyone*** was wearing them. An icon of American culture, blue jeans were born of necessity when miners' pants wouldn't stand up to the toils and daily grind of their occupation. Durable denim and heavy stitching created a riveting pant now worn worldwide. If necessity is the mother of invention, the invention's inevitable evolution will result in continual reinvention. And because of continual reinvention, I am faced with having to decide if I want faded, stone washed, regular, acid washed, torn, ripped or distressed jeans. Do I want a zipper? Once we've found my size in waist and length, I need to decide if it will be slim fit, relaxed fit, straight leg or baggy and if so what color. So many choices to make.

It may be true that according to Plato necessity is the mother of invention, and we have seen that many times throughout history. But I like to believe the path of invention is not always paved by necessity, but rather by the repurposing and reimagining of the ideas of many who came before us as we move towards a common benefit ... a path of "repurpose."

Denim pants are comfortable if you can fit in them, softening with age; it was the indigo dye that gave the pants a unique character. Indigo dye acts differently than other colors on cotton, causing the fabric to fade and wear in a unique way. As the pants fade and change you can express yourself in many ways, appearing as hardworking or casual, rebellious, informal, stylish with a jacket or downright insouciant with holes in your pants.

Reinvention and a revolt against the norm or status quo was a thing when I was a teen in the 1970s. That go big or go home mentality was reflected in our big hair and big pants. Namely, bell-bottoms became a symbol of the eccentric and colorful style of the 1970s. Bell-bottoms, pants with legs that become wider below the knee, were the pants fashion during the 1960s and 1970s. Something that was invented but certainly not out of necessity. Mom was none too pleased. Like others who were teens during the 1970s, I am thankful we at the time didn't have digital photos to forever preserve and share our fashion faux pas. Trends that move on. We truly were fashion challenged and photographs from that era enticed the same reaction, "what were we thinking?" Accessory was the Mother of invention. Add some flowers and a peace symbol embroidered on a jacket with your bell-bottomed jeans and you were hip with the times. Bell-bottoms also fit in with the new unisex style, as both men and women wore them. We watched variety shows on TV with celebrities like Sonny and Cher, James Brown, Mary Tyler Moore, or Pat Boone wearing pants tight to the knee and then flared to bells at the base dusting the floor.

Originally the invention of bell-bottom pants was due to necessity and function. Worn by sailors since the 17th century the pants could be easily rolled up to swab or mop the decks. If a sailor fell overboard, bell-bottom pants could be pulled off quickly over boots or shoes. With quick thinking, inflated bells could be a makeshift life preserver. By the 1970s bell-bottoms had become a fashion trend with our denim jeans. It was "fashion" over function as the enormous bells at the base could be a tripping hazard. It certainly was difficult to run in bell-bottom jeans, and in winter the cuffs at the base would freeze into large hoops.

I love stories. I love telling stories. The story of my life is dirty knees. It has kept me grounded through challenging times. It came in handy this past year when a crisis arrived, and in short order it seemed the world was upside down. Was this an epochal event or a reset of priorities in the inevitable ebb and flow of ups and downs? Habitual, ordinary routine is what had seemed to be normal. For many we were going through the motions. Life. Seeking purpose. Forces outside our control caused us to redefine "normal" including a cultivation of anachronistic interests previously considered outdated. And there isn't much that is as dated and old as dirt. When forced to change our way of life, it appears many others too rediscovered the joy, mental balance and aplomb provided by hands in the dirt. The gravitation towards plants is nurturing for mind, body and soul. And of course just as with people there are great histories and stories with all plants.

The picture of the plant on the cover of this book is a personal favorite. *Baptisia australis* or "false indigo" is native to North America from the Hudson Bay in Canada to the Gulf of Mexico in Texas. A hardy and herbaceous perennial, it seems to grow well in both northern and southern zones. The plant has never tried to pull the wool over anyone's eyes, so the moniker "false indigo" seems somewhat unfair. *Baptisia australis* has always been used as a dye, but considered "inferior" to dye made from "real" true indigo, *Indigofera tinctoria*, which is native to Asia. Settlers to the New World saw that Native Americans were dyeing things blue with a different kind of plant, and called it "false indigo." Not as effective as the true indigo plant, necessity is the mother of invention, so they named it false indigo and the rest is history. The Baptisia element of the name comes from the Greek root *bapto* meaning to dip or to immerse. The plant was called Baptisia because people were dipping their cloth in juice extracts. Humans throughout the years have used indigo dye to impart a lasting blue color to a wide variety of textiles. Blue is my favorite color, and considered one of the most desirable if not ***the*** most desirable color in the garden. From blue flowers to blue jeans the color has a rich history.

In the 1700s the British Empire's appetite for blue dye went well beyond the supply of Indigofera native to the West Indies. Real-life reality of supply and demand was a damper as there was too little of it to supply demand. Soon the English remembered the colonies across the ocean and learned native Baptisia could be used as a substitute. The quality was not as good but you do what you have to do. They dubbed the plant false indigo and in the spirit of commerce it became an important export. If you think the first subsidized agricultural crop in America was tobacco, corn or cotton, you would be wrong. It was the color blue as in false indigo.

From an economic standpoint the colonies output enhanced the larger British economy and supported the expansion of the British empire. What could possibly go wrong? Indigo plants couldn't be eaten, smoked, fed to animals, made into clothing, or used to build a house. But there was demand. The process of extracting the dye from the plant was costly, time consuming, and labor intensive. In 1775, South Carolina exported more than one million pounds of dried indigo cakes to England. Indigo cakes had fared better than tea during diplomatic tensions. Can you imagine a tea party demonstration with indigo dye ending up in the harbor? It would have been colorful that's for sure. Indigo business was good in 1775 but immediately was followed by a near collapse of the industry the following year. The commencement of the American Revolution put a wedge between American farmers and British customers and certainly a damper on business.

The color blue has a calming effect in the garden and in tight spaces. Baptisia today, as a landscape plant, thanks to plant breeders, has evolved into an array of color choices and varieties just like jeans that go beyond "indigo blue." And the blue jeans you're wearing are iconic and synonymous with working America analogous to a blue-collar work ethic. Plants and dirty knees. As part of the "jean pool" I need to adjust my thinking as the times change. And as a grounded individual I need to change my plants.

An explanatory kind of preamble,
Where my thoughts I begin to unscramble,
The times were tough
And we all had enough
So let's talk. I'm ready to bramble.

Chapter Two
Bramble On

FIRST THEY CAME FOR THE HOUSEhold cleaning supplies and the toilet paper. Then they came for the masks, antibacterial soap, and hand sanitizers. Then it was seeds, potting soil, bicycles, kayaks, freezers, above ground pools, puzzles and tomato plants. As store shelves cleared during the worldwide pandemic of 2020, even earthy basics like potting soil and mulch became the new toilet paper now synonymous with hoarding. Share the square became the rallying cry as store shelves emptied of available toilet paper. During the week of March 16, 2020 toilet paper sales rose 845% compared to the month prior as toilet paper became a number one seller. Not euphemistically number two anymore; it was supply and demand and the demand was off the charts. There is historical precedent for such activity and as the famous Yankee catcher Yogi Berra would say, "it's deja vu all over again." If history repeats itself toilet paper was the classic example. But why toilet paper? I'll address the reason why in chapter seven *Quintessential Normalcy*. The answers to **why** are often **rooted in history**. That includes the sudden interest in plants and gardening during a worldwide crisis.

The push to plant was reminiscent of World War I "war gardens," when President Woodrow Wilson called on the people to plant vegetable gardens to head off food shortages. A little more than 100 years later in 2020, the message resonated with a new generation of Americans fighting an invisible pandemic enemy.

During World War I and World War II, millions of Americans would "dig in to win" and helped the war effort by turning front yards, backyards, schoolyards, worksites and vacant lots into vegetable gardens. The school gardening movement arose during the Progressive Era, a time of passionate calls for reform and community improvement. Gardens were seen as a way to get city children out of crowded and unhealthy tenements, to teach them to appreciate nature, and to instill a sense of civic responsibility. The school gardening movement joined the war effort during World War I when the Federal Bureau of Education introduced the United States School Garden Army.

Charles Lathrop Pack, head of the National War Garden Commission, coined the term "victory garden" as World War I was nearing its end. The phrase was so popular it was used again during World War II. Led by the example of Eleanor Roosevelt planting a garden on the White House grounds, it was just one of the millions of victory gardens planted.

We are reminded time and again that you are never too old, never too young to try your hand at gardening. Inclusive to all age, ethnic, gender, race, creed, political affiliation or any other demographic you can think of, plants are not judgemental or political. They respond equally well or badly to anyone if properly or improperly tended. It has always been that way and always will. Gardening reinforces healthy behaviors. Researchers have suggested the level of emotional well-being, or happiness, while gardening was similar to what people reported while biking, walking or dining out. And if you vegetable garden, it takes it to yet another level when it comes to purposeful activity and quality of life.

"A Plant-demos"

Greek pándēmos of all the people, public, common, widespread + dēmos,"district, country, people"

mid 17th century: from Greek pandēmos (from pan 'all' + dēmos 'people') + -ic

During times of crisis we experience a *"**plant-demos**"* with plants, soil, growth, renewal, and a return to the garden for ***all*** people. It has been that way since the Garden of Eden itself, a place of peace and bounty, then judgment and finally a promise of restoration. The basis for a "plant-demos" play on words is the ***root*** origin of the word pandemic. The word pandemic comes from the Latin word *pandemus*, which itself comes from the Greek *pandemos*, pan meaning "all, every, whole" and dēmos, meaning "people" or ***all*** the people. "Demos" the common people, the populace in a democracy. It is evident that plants are fundamental, of intrinsic value and for ***all*** the people. In biology "deme" is a local population of organisms of the same kind, especially one in which the genetic mix is similar throughout the group. In any crisis we instinctively search our roots longing for the comfort of activities that ground us. Interaction with plants is a constitutive act. It is part of our personal constitution. If you don't believe me, look up synonyms for constitution. You will see words like vitality, essence, formation, character. Top of the list in my search for words relating to our constitution? The word ***nature.*** It's in our nature.

Sure seems like soil is in our nature. I know it's in mine. *Mycobacterium vaccae* is a non-pathogenic bacterium that lives in soil, and has shown considerable promise in health research as it relates to stress and inflammation. The idea is that as humans have moved away from farms and an agricultural or hunter and gatherer existence into cities, we have lost contact with useful microorganisms that served to regulate our immune system and suppress inappropriate inflammation. When someone brings me a suffering and failing houseplant, the first thing I do is slide it out of the pot and stick my face right in the root area. The visual inspection of the soil and roots and the aroma of the media the plant is growing in often tell us everything we need to know.

In life it's the journey itself, not always the harvest that brings about personal reward and purpose. Starting a plant from seed, turning a compost pile or growing vegetables with hands in the dirt was less an act of true self sufficiency, because growing all your own food didn't seem practical. Instead, gardening felt like alchemy. A rediscovered natural process of taking something ordinary and turning it into something naturally extraordinary, sometimes in a way that cannot be explained. ***It was about being part of the process, not just consuming.*** Purpose instead of mere consumption. Doing what should be natural is suddenly novel. To grow and share. That's what plant people do. Across the nation the focus was changing into what a young man I know referred to as a "germ-ination."

Viriditas

The comfort provided by plants certainly should not have been a surprise to us. Throughout history, plants have provided purpose and healing, and are used in analogies for our life here on earth in general. Hildegard von Bingen, born in 1098 was a German Benedictine abbess, writer, composer, philosopher and visionary. In her writings and books, she describes the scientific and medicinal properties of plants, stones, fish, reptiles, and animals. She became well known for her healing powers involving the practical application of tinctures, herbs, and precious stones.

Who wouldn't be inspired by the verdant green environs of a Benedictine monastery at the Disibodenberg in the Palatinate or Palatine forest in southwest Germany. Her monastic life as magistra of the nuns in a resplendent setting resulted in volumes of writings. Hildegard would write and speak of **"*viriditas*"** or the greening of things from within. With the turmoil and disruption of a pandemic in 2020 many people were "groaning" from within. We, of course, would call that greening from within photosynthesis. She recognized the ability of plants to absorb sunlight and transform it into energy and life. An analogy for us all. An energy to become all who you are; becoming all you can be.

> *"Good People, most royal greening verdancy,*
> *rooted in the sun, you shine with radiant*
> *light."*
>
> *– Hildegard von Bingen*

"Cornteen"

We all experienced the event we call spring in 2020 as it went on with or without us. Spring was not canceled like other events ... not even postponed. Spring was instinctively natural. When even pets and animals were at risk to catch a virus, plants proved invincible in a world-wide pandemic. And people added new words to their daily lexicon of interactions particularly in social media. For an individual unfamiliar with typing the word quarantine and spelling it properly, I saw a new fabricated word emerge. "Cornteen." Close enough. No sense correcting them, it would just go in one ear and out the other.

It seemed like the backyard birds were happy in spring 2020. It was a breath of fresh air to see all the activity at the backyard bird feeder. Was there something in the air or were we just more observant during a stay-at-home order? I saw it with

I Need to Change My Plants

Indigo buntings. Breeding males are entirely blue and make an impact when sighted. A bird with a sizable range, it winters in Central America. In the spring of 2020 its notable presence in Michigan was welcomed. Why Major League Baseball doesn't have a team named the Indigo Buntings is beyond me. If you can have cardinals, blue jays, and orioles there must be room for this mascot, considering they are in the same family as cardinals, and the bright-blue colorful caps would be very visible from the "cheep" seats. We were paying attention. You can get warblers neck craning your neck to spot a Kirtland Warbler from your backyard. We saw abundant orioles, and we saw summer tanagers outside their range enduring a "Polar Vortex" spring event. These are birds that hang out in Central America in winter while we shiver in the north. Their visit north, despite the colder than average temperatures, helped boost and grow the population of bird-watching enthusiasts.

a·nach·ro·nism

A thing belonging or appropriate to a period other than that in which it exists, especially a thing that is conspicuously old-fashioned.

Many people took up wholesome around-the-house hobbies such as baking, gardening, bird watching or herbalism, the kind of thing you do when you have "thyme" on your hands. But churning butter? Suddenly we all wanted a little Plum Creek and Walnut Grove in our lives while living at our little house on the prairie.

Reading, butter churning, candle making, and even some wildlife in the form of backyard birding while spending time at home. Birds seemed to revel in the moment with a whole new non-distracted, at-home audience during stay-at-home orders. The bluebirds, cardinals, orioles, woodpeckers and scarlet tanagers seemed to strike a pose outside our windows with a "we've been here all along" demonstration of their own.

Suddenly anachronism was the in thing. Maybe dirt, germination and plant life seemed a safe way to reconnect and live. Things as basic as washing your hands, something you were taught as a child, were given new attention.

Advances have always been met with a degree of skepticism. I remember in the 1970s the concern for living under or around power lines. Emanation from low-frequency electromagnetic fields or the cold-war worries about radiation from things like televisions, microwaves, hair dryers and electric blankets. Kids coveted an "easy bake oven" under the Christmas tree. A back to better eating habits akin to the revolt of the 1960s diet of Cool Whip, Jell-O mold salads, canned food casseroles, TV dinners and Tang. Convenience and advancement in crisis takes a backseat to good old-fashioned wholesome grounding and living. Everything slowed down.

Prior to the years of industrialization and urbanization in the late 1800s and early 1900s most Americans were farmers. Gardening for food would have seemed like an odd leisure time activity. It wasn't until the mid 1900s, with life in the suburbs and cities, that gardening would be considered nostalgic as we remembered traditional farm life.

Going off the deep end

It was an aging, 24-foot wide behemoth of thin steel and aluminum frame with liner held together by 12,000 gallons of water pressure and a few nuts and bolts: the backyard above-ground pool. With bulging metal skin you tried not to think of a collapse or split and the devastation it would have wrought on the backyard. The backyard classic or oasis in the form of an above-ground pond was floated in 1907 for the Racquet Club of Philadelphia, and was designed by bridge builders Roebling & Sons Co. By the late 1940s, post World War II sprawl spawned a marketing opportunity to middle class suburbanites and their kids, a wellspring aquifer of opportunity. A vat of chlorinated refreshment. I call it a stay-at-home "vat"-cation. A vacation oasis without ever having to leave the backyard. You could mow the lawn and after, hot and sweaty, jump into your oasis with the kids to cool off, all affordably in your own yard. In keeping up with the Jones's of the neighborhood, I sensed a stigmatization, and snubbing of above-ground pools compared to those who could afford the "in-ground" type. As a young father with 3 kids and broke, I was "gifted" a used rusty cauldron of excitement and faced the daunting task of disassembling and reassembling the 24-foot wide rusting framework. My kids learned how to swim in that pool and countless neighborhood kids sought the wellspring of my backyard benevolence. It sure created a lot of memories.

I sought backyard memories from my listening radio audience one day, and the memories of "above-ground swimming" struck a chord. One listener said, "We had one growing up. The only reason I showered in the summer was to get the chlorine off." One listener admitted to throwing fish in the pool during the fall season to give young fledgling anglers an opportunity to hook a fish. That family now has a fish story to share with others.

With social-distancing recommendations in place and public pools and water parks shuttered, restricted, the backyard above-ground pool in 2020 again became a monument erected to celebrate suburban life, liberty and pursuit of affordable summer cooling. It's as American as running through the sprinkler on a hot summer day. And with a backyard pool you didn't stub your toe scampering over the sprinkler or become twisted in a knot failing to hurdle the oscillating gusher of ice cold water in your haste. Affordable luxury I say.

When it comes to affordability there is nothing as anachronistic an activity as running I suppose. Humans have been doing it since the start of time. I've done a lot of it in my life and did more of it during the national pandemic shutdown of 2020. I personally started running in earnest during an economic crisis and downturn of 2007/2008. I realized in the midst of my problems that I was getting older and I was going to die. So I started running. It worked ... I'm still here. I also learned during long-distance runs throughout the years that distance runs are like relationships. Highs and lows and everything in between on your way to the finish line. You take it mile by mile. Some days are better than others. If you're halfway into it and hurting on a given day, you apply the 65-year-old chubby, stoop-shouldered, funny-faced man with a speech impediment known as Winston Churchill quote: "If you're going through hell keep going." I remember hot, long-distance runs where people are dropping off or throwing up by the side of the road. It messes with your head and you have to steel yourself one step at a time. You have to possess and exhibit two things: empathy and resolve. You have to visualize yourself crossing the finish line. I've had runs where someone 2 or 3 miles short of the finish line is ready to quit. You put them on your hip and talk them through the final stretch. When you cross the line you have a friend for life. I have a number of lifelong friends because I put them on my hip or they put me on their hip and we rode it out to the finish line together .... friends willing to walk through brick walls for each other.

In a world of mass transit and affordable personal transportation, some might view running as an anachronistic activity. I would assume people have done it since the beginning of time. Probably to chase their food or lamentably being chased themselves, but running nonetheless. I run multiple times each week, because I believe it keeps me mentally sharp. I noticed more people picking up the activity during the pandemic crisis to escape lockdown. In the spring of 2020 I was training for the Chicago Marathon, which eventually was cancelled due to the pandemic. During the lockdown, for the second time in my life, I was pulled over by a police officer while running. It's a strange feeling being pulled over while running. And to have it happen twice.

I was out running the trail and according to my GPS tracking watch had not yet reached my mileage goal. At the end of the trail I veered off into the parking lot of an adjoining shopping mall. This is a huge mall with an expansive parking lot. The pandemic had exacerbated the apocalypse of retail activity in malls over the past decade, and this huge expanse was eerie and silent as evening settled in. I felt small and alone as I ran around the soundless complex. I saw a police officer at the far end of the lot approaching me in his car as I ran towards him. He pulled up next to me and rolled down his window.

> "What are you doing," he said.
>
> "Running," I said.
>
> "Is that your car over there," he said.
>
> "Nope, I ran here," I said.
>
> "Do you have ID?"
>
> "No I don't carry my wallet in my shorts"
>
> "This is private property and by order of the Governor we have a stay at home order. You need to leave the premises."
>
> "I'll do my best. I can only run so fast."

I had a leg up on barefoot runners of ages past with my state-of-the-art running shoes and my GPS tracking watch. My shirt was of wicking material, technical fabrics that blend materials like polyester, elastane, spandex, and nylon. The shirt has moisture-wicking properties and even has anti-microbial properties for combating bacteria and odor. Despite these technological advances I tried to stay cool and heighten my pace as he watched me with a wary eye leave the scene of the crime. I resolved not to do that again. When you've seen one mall you've seen them "mall."

> *"It always seems impossible until it's done."*
> *– Nelson Mandela*

Maintaining a garden engages the body, mind, and senses. All three together are a win-win-win for mental and physical health. All three create a position of mindfulness ... being in the moment.

If the word "work" is a synonym for "cultivation" then I'm in for the "hoe" thing. In cultivating your attitude remember that culture, nurture and enlightenment can also be argued as closely related synonyms for cultivation. It explains why we have turned to the soil in moments of upheaval to manage our anxieties.

Gardening is the antidote to tough times, where things seem out of control. If your thoughts are a jargogle, hands in the dirt can help ground you. It is tangible and rewarding. In an age where someone can deem you as "non essential" the gardener is never without a purpose. The orderliness gardening requires, with its rules and rows, can carry over to a sense of accomplishment and purpose in a indigenous agrestal way. That seems natural. There is a risk-reward ratio inherent in gardening. Dealing with variable weather and natural threats of disease and insects that may thwart your efforts is more than counterbalanced by the reward. The redolent presence of an herb nurtured by our own hands, the promise of a ripe juicy tomato is a tangible sense of accomplishment when we're floundering around, looking for something to focus our minds on. It is why in a world of activities that vie for our attention the tomato plant or pepper plant is considered the gateway drug to gardening. Easy to grow, if you have success

I Need to Change My Plants

you will be enticed to move on to more varied and intriguing botanical forays in the future.

> Hang in there. At the very least it will inspire others.

Plan to nurture and grow, we're in this together. If we truly are in it together, then sharing our "bramblings" about life and the garden is important. Just like the brambles raspberry or blackberries, we take the thorns with the fruit, the pruning with the growth, the weeds with the sunshine each in our own patch. Bramble fruit is composed of small, individual drupes, each individual termed a drupelet, but together they form an aggregate fruit. Together they make an impact, together they are better.

These are my bramblings about the fruits of our labors. I plan to bramble on.

Rick Vuyst

I don't have a crystal ball
To help us plan protocol
We reference history
To mitigate mystery
And prognosticate for the long haul.

Chapter Three
2020 Vision

"Better to be a warrior tending to his garden than a gardener in a war."
  – Unknown Japanese Samurai saying

IMAGINE LIFE IF I WAS BORN DURING the year of 1900. It is a year of promise and possibilities as that autumn Wilbur and Orville Wright begin testing their "glider" at Kitty Hawk, North Carolina. It is also a year of disaster as thousands of lives are lost in the great storm of 1900, the Galveston hurricane and storm surge. The city of Galveston is effectively obliterated.

If I was born in 1900, by the time I am 14, I am aware of the start of World War I. Millions of both military and civilian lives are lost in the conflict that ends on my 18th birthday. The end of the war coincides with millions more dying from the Spanish Flu pandemic of 1918-1919. By my 20th birthday, millions upon millions of people have died due to the worldwide pandemic.

On my 29th birthday the stock market crashes and the Great Depression begins. In the city, people stand in long lines at soup kitchens to get a bite to eat. In the country, farmers struggle where a great drought turns the soil into dust causing huge dust storms. Apocalyptic billowing clouds of dust darken the sky, sometimes for days at a time. Crops begin to fail exposing the bare, over-plowed farmland. Eroding soil leads to massive dust storms and economic devastation. Starting in 1930 the "dirty thirties" are a difficult decade. Some people develop "dust pneumonia" and experience chest pain and difficulty breathing. The stock market loses almost 90% of its value between 1929 and 1933. Around 11,000 banks fail during the Great Depression, leaving many with no savings. In 1929, unemployment is around 3%. By 1933, it is 25%, with 1 out of every 4 people out of work. Countless businesses fail. The country nearly collapses along with the world economy.

By the time I'm 39 years old, in September of 1939, Hitler and the Nazi's invade Poland from the west. A couple days later, France and Britain declare war on Germany and another World War is under way. By the time I'm 41 an economic depression-weary U.S. is dragged into the conflict with the bombing of Pearl Harbor.

Near the close of World War II the Yalta Conference meeting of FDR, Churchill, Stalin (known as the "Big Three") occurs with the Soviet Union in control of Eastern Europe. The Cold War effectively begins and FDR is dead a few months later.

When I'm 50 a three-year conflict begins in Korea, pitting communist and capitalist forces against each other setting the stage for decades of Cold-War tension worldwide. By the time I am 62 the U.S. is increasing its involvement in Vietnam, and the Cuban Missile crisis (which epitomizes the unsteady tensions of the period) is front-page news in October of 1962. I see civil rights protests and riots during the 1960s along with the assassinations of Jack and Bobby Kennedy and Martin Luther King. When I am 69 I watch man walk on the moon. One small step for a man and a giant leap for technological advances. After the Apollo moonshots, everyday personal technology for us here on earth advances by leaps and bounds. By the time I am 75 and well into my retirement years the Vietnam war ends.

Rick Vuyst

Visual Acuity

It was Bobby Kennedy quoting his favorite poet Aeschylus who said "Even in our sleep, pain, which cannot forget, falls drop by drop upon the heart until, in our own despair, against our will, comes wisdom through the awful grace of God." I personally have always considered grace to be like water from a garden hose, it flows to the lowest point. Forgiveness itself is a form of suffering. Absorbing the debt instead of taking it out on another person. The way of crisis can be to absorb pain and not pass it on, and maintain perspective. We can rudder our thought and hold the wheel on perspective in times of trouble by understanding history.

Visual acuity is needed during times of crisis. 20/20 vision is your ability to, at a distance of 20 feet, see clearly what should normally be seen at that distance. "2020 vision" became our ability to maintain perspective, reasoning and balance when we couldn't see what was coming next. 2020 vision became the search for pellucid thought in events that were far from normal.

Understanding is rooted in history.

Others before us had gone through tough times. We would get through this too. It became evident to me that to develop navigational tools through this crisis and prepare for what's next would come from an understanding that human behavior is rooted in history.

Our lives changed in a matter of days. What was familiar was no longer an option. Free movement and commerce exchange was shut down due to a global pandemic. A silent and invisible enemy all around us was causing

> **I need to change my plants:** When you change your attitude from "I can't do this" to "I'm planting seeds" you extend to yourself grace.

serious illness as businesses shuttered their doors and turned off the lights. Words like "fluid situation" and "unprecedented" were tossed about in conversation. The exact nature of the disease and spread taking place was a point of much dubiety. Doubt sowed questions and confusion resulting in anger, fear and frustration. A real shemozzle. A kerfuffle. Unprepared for such a "war" the pandemic seemed to be winning. I reminded myself this is temporary and we will beat it.

In a dark quiet building of a closed business with no one around, my phone "pings" with a message. Someone I had never met reaching out to me in their isolation. A simple message. **"Better to be a warrior tending to his garden than a gardener in a war."**

The quote is credited to an unknown individual as a Japanese samurai phrase open to interpretation. Legend has it a Master and student went for a walk through a beautiful garden. The student questions his mentor asking, "Master, you teach me the ways of peace. I also learn from you deadly techniques of combat and the tactics of war. How do you reconcile the teaching of peace and the ways of war?" The master pauses to pluck a flower along the path and replies, "My student, it is better to be a warrior tending to his garden than a gardener in a war."

> *"Plans are established by seeking advice; so if you wage war, obtain guidance."*
> *– Proverbs 20:18 (NIV)*

I thought to myself, *change is coming.* That shouldn't be a surprise. Rainy days and storms. I picture myself in an epic battle holding a shovel. I close my eyes. I look rather ridiculous. I think *yes I'll take a garden over a war any day.* But the master wanted me to dig deeper than that. His teaching in a nutshell was ***to be prepared.*** Be resourceful and tend your garden.

It's up to you to make a difference

Generally, Grant was unflappable. During the Civil War Ulysses S. Grant one night at the Battle of the Wilderness lost his temper. Grant's officers had barged into his tent in a panic, warning him what Lee might do if they attacked.

"Oh, I am heartily tired of hearing about what Lee is going to do," Grant said. "Some of you always seem to think he is suddenly going to turn a double somersault, and land in our rear and on both of our flanks at the same time. Go back to your command and ***try to think about what we are going to do ourselves***, instead of what Lee is going to do."

It was less than a year later that Grant's armies had defeated Lee and the Civil War was over.

It's a good lesson in times of duress to think less about what someone else is going to do and focus on what you're going to do. Grant's subordinates had "paralysis by analysis," when people can't act decisively because they're so afraid to make a wrong decision.

Predict nothing. Prepare for everything.

Use of garden implements in times of war is not unprecedented. Cretan resistance was a resistance movement against the occupying forces of Nazi Germany and Italy by residents of the Greek island of Crete during World War II. It was the first time German troops had encountered mass resistance from a civilian population. The German *Wehrmacht* invaded the island in the battle of Crete, and attacking forces faced a consequential resistance from the local residents. They were "warriors in their gardens." Cretan civilians picked off Nazi paratroopers parachuting on the island with pitchforks, shovels, knives, axes, scythes or even bare hands. Many casualties were inflicted upon the invading German paratroopers during the battle.

I Need to Change My Plants

The world is on fire. Get me a garden hose.

In the decades after the horrors of World War I, many Americans remained extremely wary of becoming involved in another international conflict, and understandably so. After Germany invaded Poland in 1939, President Franklin D. Roosevelt declared that while the United States would remain neutral by law, it was impossible "that every American remain neutral in thought as well." In the 1930s, the United States Government enacted a series of laws designed to prevent the United States from being embroiled in a foreign war outlining the terms of U.S. neutrality. By the summer of 1940, France had fallen to the Nazis, and Britain was fighting virtually alone for its survival. British prime minister Winston Churchill appealed personally to Roosevelt for help. President Roosevelt agreed to exchange more than 50 outdated American destroyers for 99-year leases on British bases in the Caribbean and Newfoundland, which would be used as U.S. air and naval bases. By December with Britain's currency and gold reserves dwindling, Churchill warned Roosevelt that his country would not be able to pay cash for military supplies or shipping if America continued in a "cash and carry" approach. Roosevelt had promised to keep America out of World War II and had been re-elected based on that premise. He also understood the storm clouds gathering and wanted to support Great Britain against Germany. He began working to convince Congress and the American public that providing war materiel to Britain was in the U.S. interest.

Roosevelt's plan was the Lend-Lease Act, allowing the U.S. government to lend or lease instead of sell war supplies to any nation deemed "vital to the defense of the United States." Under this policy, the United States was able to supply military aid to its foreign allies while still remaining neutral during World War II. The Lend-Lease Act enabled a strained Great Britain to continue the fight against Germany on its own until, as we now know, the United States was drawn in late in 1941. Not only did the bombing of Pearl Harbor by the Japanese Empire change everything, Hitler added fuel to the fire by foolishly declaring war on the United States days later. Whether you believe that Japanese Admiral Isoroku Yamamoto actually said "I fear we have awakened a sleeping giant and filled him with a terrible resolve" or not, the world was on fire.

Lend-Lease prior to Pearl Harbor ran into strong opposition among isolationist members of Congress. Debate lasted for months with Roosevelt's administration and supporters in Congress arguing aid to allies like Great Britain was a necessity for the United States. As a part of his appeal, Roosevelt effectively reached into his tool box of analogies prompting him to pull out the humble, ubiquitous and yet useful common garden hose.

> *"Suppose my neighbor's home catches fire, and I have a length of garden hose four or five hundred feet away. If he can take my garden hose and connect it up with his hydrant, I may help him to put out his fire. I didn't say to him before that operation, "Neighbor, my garden hose cost me $15; you have to pay me $15 for it." I don't want $15. I want my garden hose back after the fire is over."*
>
> *– Franklin D. Roosevelt*

It was the golden age of radio. Fireside chats. When Roosevelt was first elected in 1932, forty-one percent of U.S. cities had their own radio station. Five years later nearly ninety percent of the U.S. population had access to a radio. Radio was fast overtaking newspapers as a source for news, and Roosevelt used it to his advantage as he didn't have control over what was printed in the press.

Radio gave President Roosevelt an opportunity no U.S. president had yet had: to speak directly to broad sections of the

American public without having his message filtered through the press. Presidents before him relied on reporters and editors to convey their words to the public with its editorial slant or intent out of context. It was painting pictures with words, something Roosevelt innately understood. A "whispering" into the ears of the general public via the medium of radio provided the personal effective touch complete with "earthy analogies" such as the common garden hose.

I miss the good old days.
Nostalgia isn't what it used to be.

For the lowly garden hose, both Roosevelt and ourselves have a Dutchman named Jan Van der Hayden to thank. Around 1673, the Dutch painter and inventor produced what they referred to as a fire hose. Sewing leather tubes together in 50 foot lengths allowed firefighters to get closer to a fire. The rest is history. Years later Roosevelt would use the hose in an analogy for a world on fire embroiled in another world war. I find it perfectly fitting, as grace is like water from a garden hose; it always flows to the lowest point.

During World War II shared shovels and hoes helped cultivate victory with what became known as Victory Gardens. It was a man named Charles Lathrop Pack, head of the National War Garden Commission, who coined the phrase "Victory Garden" during World War I. Credit him because it was much more positive than "War Garden" and was used again during World War II for residential plantings. These food gardens for defense were cultivated by civilians growing food to help the war effort, the troops, our allies and themselves. These gardens were located at homes, in public parks, vacant lots, baseball diamonds and workplaces. Lawns and flower beds were converted into vegetable gardens just like the automobile plants were converted over to building tanks and B24 Liberator bombers. A patriotic spirit brought agriculture to the cities. Metal which was used for war-effort munitions was in short supply, so neighbors shared garden tools like shovels and hoes. The idea of Victory Gardens contributed to both the food supply and the spirit of the people who felt they were contributing and making a difference in winning the war.

> *"Great minds discuss ideas; average minds discuss events; small minds discuss people."*
> *– Eleanor Roosevelt*

Crops and animals were commonplace around the White House in the 1800s, but, by World War II, the White House grounds were considered purely decorative. Eleanor Roosevelt fought to have a vegetable garden on the White House grounds. I'm sure Franklin Delano Roosevelt was too busy to think about planting carrots or tilling a garden. It is noted that FDR was so against the idea of an executive garden that he reportedly told others to "Tell Eleanor the yard is full of rocks or something. The people own this place, and don't want it busted up just so she can plant beans." The reality was the White House sat on what might have been the most fertile land in the city. And right on the property lived the perfect gardener. Eleanor enlisted the help of 11-year-old Diana Hopkins who happened to conveniently live at the White House as daughter to presidential advisor Harry Hopkins. Diana became the caretaker for the White House plot of beans, carrots, tomatoes, and cabbage with spade, hoe, and rake.

> *"What one has to do usually can be done."*
> *– Eleanor Roosevelt*

Young Diana played a role in cultivating a new attitude with the President. In an address a year later he said "I hope every American who possibly can will grow a victory garden this year. We found out last year that even the small gardens helped. The total harvest from victory gardens was tremendous. It made the difference." He was right. In Europe the Nazis used starvation as a weapon, a wartime tactic with blockades around the United Kingdom or during the starvation winter of 1944-1945 in Holland. Without the help of people like Diana or community victory gardens, many more people would have perished.

> *"If life were predictable it would cease to be life, and be without flavor."*
> *– Eleanor Roosevelt*

Millions of pounds of food were required by the Armed Services which put a strain on food for the homeland. Rationing and scarcity were common at home. Rationed foods included sugar, cheese, coffee, butter, milk, canned fruits and vegetables, and meat. There were national meatless and wheatless days during that time.

Families were encouraged to can their own vegetables to save commercial canned goods for the troops. In 1943, families bought 315,000 pressure cookers used in the process of canning, compared to 66,000 in 1942. The government and businesses urged people to make gardening a family and community effort.

The US Department of Agriculture estimates that more than 20 million victory gardens were planted. Fruit and vegetables harvested in these home and community plots was estimated to be 9-10 million tons, an amount equal to all commercial production of fresh vegetables. So, the program made a difference, all in the name of patriotism.

"Better to be a warrior tending to his garden than a gardener in a war." The phrase can be applied to tough times and battles and looking out for your fellow man. Tough times happen. Not *if* they will happen, but *when* they happen. Sometimes those battles are just waged with invisible enemies. If you face a battle do you know how to fight?

History often repeats itself. Warriors are those who are prepared for a repeat of the past. During World War II in the words of Winston Churchill, "Twice in a single generation, the catastrophe of world war has fallen upon us. Twice in our lifetime has the long arm of fate reached out across the oceans to bring the United States into the forefront of the battle."

> **I need to change my plants:** When you change your attitude from "I'm failing" to "I'm going to try again" you my friend are now living.

"Valleys bottom out but the sky's the limit."

Valleys bottom out but the sky's the limit. We flippantly say "such is life" when we don't have an answer for a change from our daily norm. The French say '*C'est la vie*', which equates to the English "that's life" or "life's like that." When in a difficult situation the common alternatives to the French phrase are "'that's the way it goes" or "that's the way the ball bounces" and "that's the way the cookie crumbles." *I heard time and again in 2020 that these were "unprecedented times."* But instead of waving a white flag and accepting that's the way the ball was going to bounce, much of what we were experiencing had a precedent and it would behoove us to know it, so we could in turn deal with it.

> *"If You Have a Lemon, Make a Lemonade."*
> *– Dale Carnegie*

Don't waste a crisis – your time is coming.

In 1907, Boston attorney Lawrence Luellen created a cup. It was made of paper so you could throw it away when finished drinking. In the early 1900s there were no disposable paper tissues or paper towels. You may have heard of them, Dixie cups, as they came to be known, were a novel concept and had a slow start. They didn't really get traction as a commodity for 10 years of their existence until the Spanish flu of 1918 made disposable cups a necessity. The pandemic made them a "life-saving technology" that helped stop the spread of disease.

My Mom always had a colorful communal plastic drinking cup on the kitchen sink when I was a kid. She taught us to rinse it out before using it. The habit stuck. To this day whenever I use a cup whether styrofoam, paper, plastic, glass, I find myself rinsing it out a few times before using it. A styrofoam cup fresh out of the dispenser gets my rinse-before-use treatment. My quirky behavior became a lifelong practice. My 2020 vision became an awareness that just as we were taught as kids, frequent hand washing was a learned habit grounded in common sense. And with some discipline good habits can be as difficult to break as bad habits. Just don't break the good habits.

You ain't just whistling Dixie.

Something had to be done. Tin dippers were the drinking vessel in the early 1900s and would be freely shared by many. They were communal cups. As people learned how the contagion spread, the paper cup he originally coined "the Health Kup" started to sell. Luellen and his business partner Hugh Moore are the perfect example of if you don't succeed try, try again. Scrap, survive, adjust and hang in there until the timing is right. Drinking out of a disposable cup became a matter of life and death. The paper cups were not built to last, but the idea sure was. Drink. Toss. Repeat.

In response, Luellen and Moore launched an advertising campaign to drive the point home and rebranded from the Health Kup to the more memorable Dixie cup in 1919. The entrepreneurial vessels were as reliable as old ten-dollar bills (from the French dix meaning ten) issued by Louisiana prior to the Civil War. Their function, purpose and use were reliable. And pioneering the product opened the door to a wave of single use or disposable items like razors.

Changing the name to Dixie cup in 1919 they developed a free-standing dispenser that was sold to businesses. The two began dispensing individual servings of water for a penny—one cent for a five-ounce cup from a tall, clumsy porcelain water cooler.

Once a business bought a dispenser, Luellen and Moore could depend on revenue from the repurchase of cups. It introduced the paper cup to thousands of workers who would naturally then buy them in stores for home use. Eventually homeowners bought dispensers for the bathroom to amend their nightly before-bed brushing habit.

A paper cup is a novel idea and the creators probably took some ribbing before it caught on. But creative containment and distribution of water was not a new concept. The first commercially distributed water in America was bottled and sold by Jackson's Spa in Boston in 1767. Early drinkers of bottled spa waters believed that the water at these mineral springs had therapeutic properties and that bathing in or drinking the water could help treat many common ailments. Visits to natural springs and spas became fashionable among the wealthy elite during the 19th and early 20th centuries. Poland Spring was a celebrated inn built way back in 1797. In the mid 1800s Hiram Ricker, grandson of the Ricker family that built the inn in Maine, believed the spring water there benefited his health. Legend has it Hiram Ricker claimed that spring water from the property cured him of chronic dyspepsia, better known as good old indigestion. The American bottled water industry had its start from the perceived remarkable therapeutic properties of water from a local spring and the rest is history.

Don't waste a crisis. Your time is coming.
Learn to adapt and meet the moment.

I quote a friend of mine, a Marine. He served overseas in the 2nd Battalion, 5th Marines, a historic battalion for its reputation, professionalism and performance. One of the most decorated in history, the 2nd battalion, 5th Marines found themselves wherever the Marine Corps was making history.

Their battalion motto is "Retreat? Hell, we just got here" and comes from the 1918 World War I battle of Belleau Wood.

He is a Marine that has engaged in gunfights on the streets of Ramadi, Iraq. He has described to me his experience battling insurgents in the streets. In one case the insurgents were shooting at him and his fellow Marines with RPGs. Near the Humvee he remembers clearly the feeling of the moment. An explosion, it felt like someone had just punched him in the face. Pulled around to the backside of the Humvee by his lieutenant, he was bleeding heavily from his upper lip. They pulled the metal out of his upper lip and slowed the bleeding. Shrapnel was removed from his leg. Matthew received a Purple Heart for being wounded in action.

In the midst of the turmoil in 2020 Matthew said this, and when he talks I pay attention. "There are all types of storms. Different generations experience different types. This is not the first time our country has experienced a storm. They blow through from time to time to remind us that even WE are vulnerable. That even WE must batten down the hatches for rough seas. The only guarantee about a storm is that it will eventually pass and bring sunny skies. Unrest, uncertainty, anger and division. We are all in this storm together. The only way to get through this is to recognize and respect the storm for what it is. It is here to beat us up, push us around, teach us a lesson and to make us stronger by eventually uniting us. When this storm passes I can guarantee one thing ... we might be beat up, frayed and bent over.....but WE will always remain standing with the sun shining on our backs. Our foundation is unbreakable. There is no storm too powerful to break us."

He is right. In a pandemic we may be isolated but we are not alone.

In this crisis to hit the pause button and reorient, prioritize, reflect. To rest from the maddening pace the world was on. It was Ovid the Roman poet who said, "Take rest; a field that has rested gives a bountiful crop."

There is an opportunity to choose dedication over drama; to be well grounded in a crisis; to tend to your garden. I would seek grounding and do some self inquiry rooted in experiences from my younger days. As I charted and plotted my way forward I decided I would navigate my inner "*Fra Mauro*" inspired by a 15th-century Venetian monk. There has to be something there from my days of youth. Isn't that what a psychologist would do? I would seek advice from a few elder "Oakleys" for insight. I wasn't about to waste a crisis.

I found my footing and decided it's better to be a warrior tending to his garden than a gardener in a war.

My purpose I worked to find
Not much had been designed
In my much younger days
I went through a phase
To understand theatre of the mind

Chapter Four
My Fra Mauro Formation

REMEMBER MY DAD'S VEGETABLE GARden. As a kid it seemed huge. Giant tomato plants. Gargantuan rhubarb leaves and row after row of carrots. So many weeds. Rows and rows of beans. Always work to be done. I went back years later and the garden is just an unused small patch. Did you ever have the experience of returning to the house you grew up in? Did it feel like the house and its rooms were much smaller than they seemed when you were a child? That you grew up but the home never did? Do you remember the backyard as very large only to discover, as an adult, how small it really was? I sold my parents home when they were ready to move to a condominium. The rooms in the house felt small and nothing like I remembered them to be as a child. Usually going back to a childhood home is a disappointment. Still there is much to be learned by revisiting the plots of our younger years. The memories and the experiences truly are larger than life. You learn as you age to put things in perspective, and what seemed so "big" years ago is now just a small piece of your puzzle.

As a young boy I was "drafted" by my Mom and Dad into a program for boys and teens called "Cadets." We wore grey shirts and "kerchiefs" and were subject to inspections or review of our attire, uniform and posture at each meeting. Kerchiefs were a square of cloth worn around the neck. We would recite our creed and stand at attention to say the pledge of allegiance. I remember standing straight and hoping my shirt was tucked, zipper up and kerchief securely cinched to my neck. The "head counselor" would walk the floor like a drill sergeant, carefully inspecting each cadet for violations. This was a man who would do everything by the book. Everything was scheduled, in its place, spotless clean and accounted for even in his personal life. The lawn, windows, garage and vehicles at his house were meticulous. If not dressed to code you would receive a "demerit." There would be some sort of "demerit" comeuppance if you forgot your kerchief, a common occurrence. We were young and impressionable and recited the cadet code every week. I can still recite it some 50 years later.

> A Cadet must be:
> reverent,
> obedient,
> compassionate,
> consecrated,
> trustworthy,
> pure,
> grateful,
> loyal,
> industrious
> cheerful

Oh that's all? Why don't we throw in dauntless, perfect, fearless, philanthropist, astute, genius and gregarious while we're at it. Looking back, that's quite a lot of pressure on a 10-year-old kid. Even at the age of 60 I'm struggling on a number of those on that list to be honest with you. I remember thinking as a kid,

Okay, I'll give it a shot but don't count on a 100% score. My demerits alone are going to tamp down that final score.

When you earned a badge your Mom would sew it on your shirt so you could display it proudly at the next inspection. There was pressure on her too as there was proper placement protocol and attachment criteria. The pressure was compounded by a young boy's proclivity to wait until just before you're going to leave for a meeting to ask her to sew it on. Don't be late. You're liable to get a "demerit" and arrive for inspection with your kerchief askew. I lived in fear of demerits. As I advanced in the program I would proudly wear the stripes on my sleeve as I moved up the ranks.

It was there I began my love for photography as each boy was loaned a "brownie" camera, and we learned how to manage and develop film in a dark room. The Brownie was a long-running popular series of simple and inexpensive photo cameras made by Kodak. It introduced the point and click snapshot to the masses. Brownies were extensively marketed to kids like me, with Kodak using them to popularize photography. They were also taken to war by soldiers. As they were ubiquitous, many iconic shots were taken on Brownies. I can still smell the aroma of the strange chemical bath agents we floated the film in while operating in the dark, hoping our black and white prints would be a success. We were playing with ammonium thiosulfate and sodium thiosulfate in the dark as children. I was operating in the dark literally and figuratively making it up as I went to earn the coveted merit badge. I didn't want to be exposed for my questionable skills. I remember a thermometer at the ready to gauge the temperature in the tray. I inadvertently licked it off to clean it once while focused and working in the dark. I thought I was going to die but I didn't dare tell anyone. My life flashed before my eyes. I survived. Obviously.

The highlight of my years in the ranks was when we could jointly as a team build a motorized go cart. We would craft a metal frame and position the remnants of a metal lawn chair pilot seat in the center as we devised a cockpit. With the help of our counselor, we would secure a used lawnmower engine and steering wheel from the local rummage lot. Still a few years removed from our driver's permits and high school, this was a big deal for a 13-year-old. It represented freedom. The open road. A passage into manhood. From the start I questioned the integrity of that grease-soaked engine, but our counselor was on a budget and he got it cheap. Must be the dues collections were a little short that month. We bolted that symbol of Henry Ford's combustible imagination to the rear of the frame and wired the control components to the cockpit. Weeks turned to months but finally this modern marvel of 20th century junior automation was ready to launch.

Due to my rank exhibited by the stripes on my sleeve and lack of personal demerits I was designated the "John Glenn" distinction of manning the maiden voyage. I took off the kerchief and with the help of jealous onlookers was strapped into the cockpit. This would be my finest moment in front of my fellow cadets. We were young men from the Apollo generation and failure was not an option. It was 1972 and our heroes were the likes of Neil Armstrong. Instead, in my little world it was a near disaster like Apollo 13, and I would narrowly miss my "Fra Mauro" landing while avoiding personal ruination.

Fra Mauro was a Venetian cartographer, monk and mapmaker. In his youth, Mauro had traveled extensively as a merchant and a soldier. In the records of his monastery his main job was collecting the monastery's rents, but he is also known as the creator of a series of world maps. Later in life he no longer traveled due to his religious and monk status, but would frequently consult with merchants of the city upon their return from overseas voyages. He managed to compose a great "*mappa mundi*" or world map. It was the most detailed and accurate map of the world up until that time, the Fra Mauro map. He made it his life's work to chart the course of merchants and travelers in order to create the most definitive map of the world. Accounts from travelers interviewed by the monk were used in the plotting of the map. It is said "no sailor's tale was too mundane or merchant chart too crude" for Fra Mauro.

*Fra Mauro understood **everyone has a story.***

The crater Fra Mauro and the Fra Mauro surface on the Moon are named after him. The Apollo 13 lunar mission had intentions to explore the Fra Mauro formation, but due to the explosion of an oxygen tank in the service module and the ensuing crisis, Apollo 13's crew had to return to Earth without landing on the Moon. I remember the news updates as a child as the unfolding saga played out in April of 1970. The Fra Mauro formation was instead explored by astronauts Alan Shepard and Edgar Mitchell of the Apollo 14 mission in February 1971. The 80-kilometer diameter crater Fra Mauro was regarded as interesting scientifically to understand the moon's geologic history. The crater served as a natural drill hole to allow the astronauts to obtain imbrium ejecta from the surface. Ejecta, essentially the surface blanketed by the impact forming the crater, is vocabulary I intend to use from now on when digging a hole to plant a tree or shrub. Somehow ejecta sounds so much more exciting than a dirt pile.

The command module pilot for Apollo 14 was Stuart Roosa. When I was 11 years old Astronaut Stuart Roosa, a former U.S. Forest Service smokejumper, carried about 500 tree seeds into space as part of the three-man Apollo 14 crew. Upon their return to Earth, the seeds were germinated, and most of the seedlings were given away to be planted as part of 1976 bicentennial celebrations across the country. While commander Alan Shepard was hitting golf balls in space, command module pilot Stuart Roosa was carrying future generations of tree seeds into orbit. One such tree, with the help of local native President Gerald Ford found its way to West Michigan. Unfortunately the tree in later years was mistakenly cut down in a landscaping mishap. In 2009 I partnered with the Wyoming Police department to bring another descendant of Roosa's sycamore trees back to West Michigan. We planted the tree, complete with a ceremony attended by NASA and US Forest Service representatives and other dignitaries, an offspring of a first generation Moon tree which today stands on the grounds of the Wyoming, Michigan Police department.

Now with images of my heroes the Apollo astronauts in my thoughts, my counselor put his foot on the rear of the cart and gave the pull chord on the engine a yank. It sputtered. The head counselor with arms crossed watched from his perch on the front steps of our meeting building. Jolted by his successive pulls the engine belched and finally with a puff of black smoke it roared to life. Roar would be an exaggeration but it was functioning nonetheless. Over the din of the engine directly behind my seat I heard him say "Good luck and Godspeed" as he stepped away from the shuddering frame. It was a fall evening and the parking lot we were in was dark and damp at the end of an October day.

Taking a deep breath I released the brake. Throttle up. I had underestimated the life that remained in that old lawnmower engine. Lurching forward I was quickly up to full speed. The parsonage of the church that shared that parking lot was dead ahead and I was closing fast. I knew I didn't want to be a news item in the following Sunday's church bulletin, so I pulled the wheel hard left. Skidding along the wet pavement I fought the wheel to coax the frame from impending disaster.

Managing the turn at high speed I tried to brake. No brakes. Fighting the G forces on my second turn I reached for the throttle. It was stuck. I managed a third turn and the crowd of onlookers scrambled for cover. I saw my "counselor" running towards me and yelling something unintelligible. He couldn't catch me due to my rate of speed and his 3-pack-a-day Marlboro habit. I couldn't hear him due to the din of the engine. I surmised I could fight the G forces and continue to make turns until it ran out of gas. That could be more than an hour. The shuddering frame could break apart from pressures. I thought *Abort! Abort! Abort!* I couldn't reach for the buckle, I had to keep both hands on the wheel to fight centrifugal force. I realized at this point my only recourse was to take the hurdling mass into the wall ... to take one for the team.

Suddenly, I saw an outcropping of parking lot bumper blocks. I made a snap decision to use them instead of the north wall of our cadet building. I could reduce my "demerits" by slamming the approaching curb bumpers instead of the building where the head counselor resides. I hit the first row at full speed and much to my surprise and chagrin it sent this pilot and his craft airborne. The second row of bumper blocks brought the errant mass to an abrupt stop as the crumpled frame and lawn chair cockpit crashed and lodged on the concrete. The engine was still at a full roar. By then the rescue cadets had arrived to hit the kill switch on the engine while I pulled to unlatch my seat buckle. The physical pain was far less than the hurt feelings as I was subject to uproarious laughter stepping away from the smoking wreckage. The head counselor was still standing on the steps with arms crossed. I could picture him tearing off my stripes at the next inspection. My fellow cadets were bent over in laughter at my misfortune as I emerged from the cockpit. I had failed, was told so, and would never live down my crash landing. But just like my dark room chemical experience I had survived it and lived for another day. I walked away from the wreckage. Lesson learned. I would walk away from a number of wrecks over my lifetime.

While a "cadet" I was also taught knot tying under the guise it would come in handy someday and earn me a "merit badge." It was certainly safer than chemical formulations and internal combustion engines. We struggled to craft the clove hitch, square knot, bowline and other knots, and, upon completion, mount them on a varnished board in the shape of a shield to hang on the wall. We used the old clunky label makers called "Dymo" label makers to identify our knots and accept compliments from family and friends, mostly Mom and Dad, on our ligature prowess. We varnished the knots to a hardened state, because if I untied them today I would never be able to re-tie the knot. Looking back I would say the only benefit I derived from the experience and kerchief conundrum is a life-long skill at tying a crisp, tight professional necktie on a clean, starched white shirt.

Even today anyone who knows me well knows I can tie a great necktie but if my car breaks down I'm lost. Looking back I think that experience was the foundation of my disdain for small engine maintenance and repair. Small engines are handy around the home, but if my lawnmower, generator, snowblower, leaf blower or weed whacker won't start on the first or second pull I'm pretty much out of luck. I would open the hood and look for a big on/off switch that was switched off. If I can't find that I'm out of luck. Thank goodness for the advent of cell phones and on-line instructional videos.

Thankfully after Cadets I made it to high school alive and managed to hone my skills for dramatics. I found my sweet spot, my calling. As a teen I loved trees and plants, dramatics and history. The big change for me took place in March of 1977. I was cast in a dramatic performance as Teddy Brewster, the beloved crazy brother of two crazy sisters, who believes he is President Teddy Roosevelt.

> *"Speak softly and carry a big stick; you will go far."*
> — *Theodore Roosevelt*

Theodore Roosevelt is often considered the "conservationist president." On June 8, 1906, President Theodore Roosevelt signed the Antiquities Act into law establishing the first general legal protection of cultural and natural resources in the United States. The act set important precedents, including the assertion of a broad public interest in archeology on public lands, care and management of sites, collections, and information. The act linked the protection of natural sites with public programs to care for these natural resources.

Conservation increasingly became one of Roosevelt's main concerns. After becoming president in 1901, Roosevelt used his authority to protect wildlife and public lands by creating the United States Forest Service (USFS) and establishing national forests, federal bird reserves, national game preserves, national parks, and national monuments. It would be years later as Governor of California that another future president, Ronald Reagan, would be vilified for a quote regarding the proposal to create Redwood National Park, "A tree is a tree. How many more do you have to look at?"

It was J. Sterling Morton the father of Arbor Day who said, "Each generation takes the earth as trustees."

President Roosevelt caught on to this and in a proclamation to school children in 1907 said "A people without children would face a hopeless future; a country without trees is almost as hopeless; forests which are so used that they cannot renew themselves will soon vanish, and with them all their benefits. ***A true forest is not merely a storehouse full of wood, but, as it were, a factory of wood*** and at the same time a reservoir of water. When you help to preserve our forests or to plant new ones, you are acting the part of good citizens. The value of forestry deserves, therefore, to be taught in the schools, which aim to make good citizens of you. If your Arbor Day exercises help you to realize what benefits each one of you receives from the forests, and how by your assistance these benefits may continue, they will serve a good end."

Teddy

I jumped at the chance to play the role of Teddy Roosevelt my senior year of school in the big annual production. My moment had arrived and I was about to blossom. I would star alongside two crazy fun-loving ladies, Abby Brewster and Martha Brewster, two elderly sisters who accidentally fell into the practice of "soothing" the loneliness of old men by killing them off with their personalized recipe for elderberry wine.

The year is 1941 and the location is a small house next to a cemetery in Brooklyn. In this house the thoughtful, sweet old ladies, Martha and Abby Brewster have developed a very bad habit. The sisters doctor the punch bowl adding arsenic, strychnine and just a pinch of cyanide to each gallon of elderberry wine. Abby and Martha perceive what they do as charity. My job in the production of *Arsenic and Old Lace* is to be put to work in the basement known as Panama or the Panama Canal burying the gentlemen in a hand dug trench called "digging a loch." The aunts enlist me to take the victims to the Panama Canal (the cellar) and bury them.

> *"If you could kick the person in the pants responsible for most of your trouble, you wouldn't sit for a month."*
> – *Theodore Roosevelt*

In one of the scenes of the production Aunt Martha becomes concerned for a Mr. Hoskins, one of their elderberry wine victims, who has been "patiently waiting in the window seat." Aunt Abby believes it would be a good idea for me to get him downstairs right away. The sisters agree to wait until guests in the home have gone to bed to have the "services" for Mr Hoskins in the basement.

In the scene I am reporting to the aunties that the General is very pleased because the Canal is just the right size.

Abby at this point interrupts to declare, "Teddy! Teddy, there's been another Yellow Fever victim."

My response as Teddy Roosevelt is, "Oh, dear me. This will be a shock to the General. But I'll have to tell him. Army regulations, you know."

At this point Abby and Martha insist I keep it a secret which is intriguing to me. "A state secret?"

The aunts reply, "Yes, a state secret. Promise?"

I loved the aunties who took care of me, especially the biscuits and tea they would treat me with. "You have the word of the President of the United States. Cross my heart and hope to die."

At this point the aunties instruct me to take the corpse down to the basement and they would come down later to hold services.

Me: "You may announce that the President will say a few words."
Whispering to the aunts I say, "Where is the poor devil?"
Aunt Martha: "He's in the window seat."
Me: "Oh. Seems to be spreading. We've never had Yellow Fever there before."

> *"Keep your eyes on the stars, and your feet on the ground."*
>
> *– Theodore Roosevelt*

The next scene changed my life forever. With an understood yet unspoken carte blanche nod from the production's director, I proceeded to improvise and exaggerate the dramatics with the stage all to myself. Technically I shared the stage with Mr Hoskins stiff dead body and didn't speak a word. But I was determined to speak softly and carry a big stick. In this case a big stiff from the parlor window seat to his final resting place the Panama canal.

The stage was darkened to dim lights that cast spooky shadows on the parlor of lace curtains, heavy fabric furniture and the aunties dirty deeds. I emerge from the basement with a squeak of the door and stand perusing the scene with arms crossed. The theatre was full but from my vantage point you could not see the audience because of the spotlights piercing the darkness shining into my eyes. But oh could you hear them. Giggles, laughter and gasps from the audience filled the theatre as I cautiously made my way from the basement door to the parlor window seat. With a creaking noise I pry open the window seat and step back at the sight of poor Mr. Hoskins prone and stiff filling the seat. I could have simply picked him up and carried him back to the basement, but this was my moment to speak softly and carry a big "stiff."

For the next few minutes I own the stage, attempting to lift Mr Hoskins from the seat and move him to the canal. In a series of antics and missteps I "dance" with Mr Hoskins, including a flop on the couch with the corpse on a dimly lit stage. By the time I made it to the basement steps, the theatre rang with the sound of guffaws, laughter, cheering and applause. Each night of the production I strung out the scene utilizing what I had found to entice a crowd reaction. By closing night of the production I had it down cold, no pun intended, and milked the dramatics to a packed house. It was a feeling of power and control theatrics that would sometimes help me and sometimes hurt me the rest of my life. But I was hooked. Even today as I do my radio show I often think "theatre of the mind" as we "perform" painting pictures with words to a microphone and an audience we can't see. An understanding that we ***think*** in pictures we ***speak*** in words.

Digging in the backyard

As an example, with my built-in flair for dramatics, it would be years later I would find myself in a real-life backyard scene. In Michigan, winter starts early, and the yard expeditions for a plant lover are hampered by lack of light. Daylight Saving

Time. Time and again in the dark I have had to use a pick axe to break through the upper crust of November frost in the ground to plant a bargain. This with the aid of enlightenment. No, not the European and colonial intellectual movement cultivated in the late 17th and 18th centuries emphasizing reason and individualism rather than tradition. No, flashlights and spotlights casting shadows on the frozen tundra after dark. Planting in the "off-seasons" in the dark became tradition with me, much to the entertainment value of the surrounding neighbors who would peek through the blinds or curtains to observe my antics.

One early winter evening my neighbor came home from work pulling into the driveway. There I was in the yard with a flashlight, snow shovel, garden shovel, wheelbarrow, hatchet and a pick axe. He paused a moment as he cautiously stepped out of the car and straightened himself warily observing from a distance. I was filthy, covered in dirt and snow holding a pick axe. Because of the cold temperatures I had one of those black pull-over balaclava masks that people wear when robbing a bank or a liquor store. I had dropped my flashlight, and, it with the street light, cast long dark elongated and eerie unearthly shadows across the snow. The Moon silhouetted the branches of the trees casting dark-fingered shadows across the white surface, and the air was frosty and perfectly calm. We stood in embarrassed silence, looking at each other with only the sound of our breathing and the mist of our breath filling the air. We stood in surprised silence for what seemed like 5 minutes just looking at each other. Instead of trying to explain, I decided to proceed with the pick axe to plant my discounted tulip bulbs, and he quietly and briskly stepped into his home never taking his eyes off me in the process. We never discussed the moment or talked again, and he moved a few months after the event. To this day I'm sure he thinks I'm a serial killer.

The Ejecta Button

Today the thought of knot tying two half hitches and a sheet bend knot for merit badges returns to my memory as I ruminate on the "denouement" of my youth and its adventures. Denouement comes from the French for "untying" or "unknotting," as in untying a knot; it's the metaphor for a climax, where the plot is unraveled. I learned from my personal experience and from other guys my age and older that at 60 there is a measure of leveling off. You also, along with your friends, become very aware that when you turn 60 the check engine light comes on. They say when you near the end of your rope you tie a knot in it and hang on. You eventually land at your Fra Mauro. I call it pushing my "ejecta" button. When the dust of ejecta settles on your Fra Mauro, the change that takes place is this: your drive is replaced by more measured wisdom. But I don't want to just "settle" or hang on. The fascination, the learning, desire for adventure and the enchantment with change doesn't go away. The wonder never, never goes away. You just move a little slower. It's the theatre of the mind now playing in my head. You don't have to have all the answers. If you're not befuddled, you're not asking the right questions and living to the fullest. Bravo. The show must go on.

Rick Vuyst

When your direction is switched
And plans effectively glitched
There along your path
And in the aftermath
Your life's forever enriched

Chapter Five
Oakley Oracles

On an April evening I took a walk down the path from my house to Lake Michigan. The fog was so thick if you didn't know your way you could find yourself walking in circles. Piercing the murk and mist were the distant intermittent mournful sounds of a foghorn in the channel, providing audible direction for mariners shrouded in grey. Navigating by sound is less than ideal, and often a tricky way to maneuver during reduced visibility. You do what you have to do. Ironic, because that's how foggy my mind felt at the time.

A common occurrence in spring on the big lake, when moist warmer air blows across lake water temperatures that are still "winter cold" and around 45 degrees, a thick fog forms and rolls off the lake. You can become engulfed by the fog as I was by the questions in my mind. I didn't have answers. I wasn't in a war, but in April 2020 with more questions than answers, it certainly felt like fog. The word "fog" in reference to uncertainty in war was coined and credited to Prussian military general Carl Phillip Gottfried von Clausewitz as he sought skilled counsel to scent out the truth in the midst of chaos.

I Need to Change My Plants

There on my path in the thick fog was the furrowed massive trunk of a favorite oak tree that had weathered many lakeshore storms and seasons. A tree of sizable circumference, two people would not be able to even come close to wrapping their arms around its girth. Oaks tend to grow taller than other trees, and have a long life span; this one I guessed to be well over 100 years old, and, due to its proximity to the shoreline, looked weathered and even older. I have conversations with the tree from time to time, because it looks wise, and, to be honest with you, is a good listener. I do most of the talking. The tree I surmised and imagined had seen its share of battles. The huge sweeping canopy in the fog looked like tattered sails and ropes of a masted schooner fighting the waves of storms and elements.

You can laugh at the fact I talk to a tree or plants for that matter, but keep in mind before passing judgement that roughly 20 to 25 percent of waking time is spent on conversation with ourselves. Plants actually give us opportunity for expatiation of the burdens we carry. If you maintain a discourse for more than 25% of the day with yourself, the next logical step would be to talk to your plants. It's a confidence-building reassurance that I'm OK you're OK. And plants and flowers are very visual. Remember, we think in terms of pictures, but we speak with words. That's what I've loved about doing live broadcast radio for over a quarter century. We paint pictures with our words.

It is theorized that oaks, with a deep central root as well as the cell structure nature of the cambium under the bark of the oak's trunk, make it a target for lightning. These issues make oak trees better conductors and better "grounders of lightning" than trees with shallow roots. On a moonlit foggy evening the gnarled branches and the shadows they cast look legendary in my imagination. It's not only the massive size and the battles this tree has survived, it's the legendary status of oaks that draw me to this tree.

Oak trees live for a long time. Throughout history people connected this longevity to wisdom and sought the shade of oak trees when making important decisions. Gatherings would take place below its branches and disputes settled. Perceived wisdom exuded from the tree would help them resolve disputes fairly. And because the oak species is one of the last to shed its leaves in fall and winter, ancient cultures would view this as a sign of determined, dogged, steadfast will and determination. For this reason, oak leaves came to symbolize victory in battle. Generals were presented with wreaths made of oak leaves after important battles. Native American chiefs often held important meetings around a Council Oak.

And then there is the "Major Oak" where Robin and his Merry Men would meet in Sherwood Forest: a large English *Quercus* near the village of Edwinstowe in the middle of Sherwood Forest, Nottinghamshire, England. It was Robin Hood's shelter where he and his merry men slept. And according to folklore, Robin had all the components of effective leadership. He had a vision and a plan. He surrounded himself with effective people. He inspired those people. He appreciated his people for the unique individuals they were.

Beyond the fog is clarity.

In the midst of the fog I decide to seek out more Oakleys in my life ... to harvest wisdom. I didn't need to know all the answers ... I just needed the right answers.

Thomas Jefferson once said that while he was an old man, he was yet a young gardener, with still so much to learn. There are gardens to grow, seeds to sow, trees to plant and relationships to nurture. As we do this we reflect like Jefferson on the finiteness of our own lifespan. If we can balance inevitable change with well-grounded unshakable virtues and beliefs, we temper some of the sadness of time wasted and opportunities squandered. We make a difference. It's called gaining wisdom from your experience and cultivating it for the good of others. It's growing purpose and relevance. It's becoming an Oakley. Alexander Hamilton said it best in the Broadway musical *Hamilton*: "Legacy. What is a legacy? It's planting seeds in a garden you never get to see."

Hiding in the Basement

Theodore Szczepanski is 104 years old. He's a lot like my friend Oakley, the 100-plus-year-old weathered oak that I talk to on my path, only Ted's more talkative. With Oakley I'll admit I do most of the talking. Both have been through a lot and have stood the test of time. Both are weathered and wise. Both have a purpose on this earth. I am thankful both are in my path.

> Oakley. *adjective.* The ability to influence others in a positive way with your standing and experience.

You ask Ted a question and it ignites a thought which turns into a story. Ted will start a story, which starts another story path, which has a background story for perspective, until he playfully taps his forehead and can't remember "where he was going with this." Ted will do that as you sit on the edge of your seat trying to draw the details from him. He apologizes saying it never used to happen to him until he "got old." I have other very seasoned friends who do the same. I'm convinced I'll be like that, I'm already doing it. Abandoning the initial thought, we then begin a quizzical journey down another road. That's the beauty. Ted is just like those aging majestic trees in fall ... they become more colorful as the season ages.

Some trees are more colorful, making the most of the seasons they are given. Consider one of my all-time-favorite trees Juneberry. Native to North America, it goes by a lot of names like Amelanchier, serviceberry, shadberry, sarvis, sarvisberry, snowy mespilus, chuckley pear, and Saskatoon to name a few. It makes the most of every season given to it. Gorgeous white blooms in spring, delicious nutritious edible berries in June, fabulous fall color; then they rest as a deciduous tree in winter. Seems like a good life for a tree. If you haven't talked to a tree you should try it. It's therapeutic. They are good listeners. If you haven't spent time with some centenarians in your path you should try that too. The oracles of these "Oakleys" can ground your thinking and help you reset your navigation.

A friend of mine who has a 106-year-old Grandma shares with me her theory on longevity. When asked what the secret was to a long happy life she simply replied with two words. A total of 5 letters. "Do you." Brilliant. Be yourself and follow your path.

A Sagacious Centenarian

Ted leans back in his chair and collects his thoughts. He insists the reason he is here today, after close to 38,000 days on earth, is that he lived a healthy life and didn't pick up bad habits at a young age.

He mentions it a couple times causing me to ask, "why does that stick out in your mind Ted?"

"I guess it's because no one ever encouraged me to try, I wasn't enticed to take up the habit even though at a game of cards everyone was smoking." He taps the side of his head with a finger to illustrate he instinctively knew it wasn't the right course for him even then. He was following his own path and "Someone was looking over me," says Ted.

You see, with Ted, first and foremost when listening to the hesternal thoughts from this centenarian, he is convinced that there is someone looking over us. That someone is placed in your path at just the right time to steer you back on course. When you "Do you" everyone needs a little well-timed course adjustment.

"God?" I ask Ted.

I Need to Change My Plants

He nods his head. Holding out his hands he creates imaginary paths with his fingers. He takes one finger and quisitively watches a finger veer off course from the other 9. He then says someone is there to set him straight, demonstrating by drawing his hands together in a prayerful position.

"You see at the right moment someone is there in your path," says Ted nodding.

I question Ted just like the imaginary friend in my mind, *Quercus*, who stops to ask questions of the big old oak tree on our path.

The next time I visit Ted it's two fingers in the shape of a V. Similar to what people would call the peace sign or victory sign. He watches as he uses his free hand and traces a path up one finger and part way says, "whoops wrong way!" and backtracks to head up the other finger.

Whenever life gets difficult, a decision is to be made or things suddenly veer off course, someone is placed in your path. Someone to help redirect your course. Someone to help you discover answers. A presence I thought. Just like the big old oak tree on my path that listens to me talk.

"Some people are going to question your theory Ted," I say to him.

"Oh, you don't have to see the people placed in your path," Ted says. "That's your choice. But they are there for everyone. The signs are everywhere. Your job is to choose to see them."

> *"Between every two pine trees there is a door leading to a new way of life."*
> *– John Muir*

Ted tells me his story. He was a POW for a period of time during World War II. He was captured in the area of Ukange and Bertrange France, two communities split by the Moselle river and less than an hour's drive west of the German border.

As the Germans overran the area, the Allies were trapped and hid in the basements of homes. The intransigent Germans flushed those hiding in the area by moving house-to-house with tanks and flattening the abode. Ted and his 10 or so comrades hid and survived in a basement for a couple days and had a decision to make. Their current position was not sustainable. Do they, under the cover of darkness, break for the meadow of grasses behind the home and run for cover in the woods beyond the field? Or do they surrender? They opted to surrender during daylight knowing if found out at night they would be unconditionally shot. If they surrendered before sunset with hands up they would be prisoners, but their odds of surviving were better.

As they emerged from the basement with hands up the bewildered and flabbergasted Germans stood with mouths open in amazement. Where did these guys come from? I laugh as Ted reenacts the looks on the faces of the soldiers.

"Do you think they showed you some measure of compassion as humans?" I asked Ted.

"After their shock I suppose so," says Ted.

Emerging from the basement and in the light of day "we could see we had collectively made the right decision. The meadow and the woods edge were covered by machine gun nests for anyone who might opt for our considered option of a night-time run. We would have never made it. I wouldn't be sitting here today."

They were sent to a prison. That was followed by a second prison. Most of the POWs were used as labor for road construction repair. Europe by that time was war torn and roads had to be fixed. It was hard work with little nutrition as the daily menu of POWs was a couple of small pieces of bread a day. That's where Ted's theory kicks in, the "someone in your path" theory.

One of the guys in his group of POWs, a person in Ted's path and friend at that moment, had an idea. Have the sergeant ask the Germans if they could be put on farm duty instead of road duty. Miraculously it worked and Ted believes it saved him.

I Need to Change My Plants

They went to work on a farm where there was food. Sure they had to steal some of it. Sure they had to work hard. They stole food from the pigs. They ate potatoes intended for the pigs. They survived. I pose the question to Ted, "what if" your friend the POW had not been there in the right place at the right time to plant the seed that they work on a farm for their captors? Ted shrugs his shoulders. What if?

When I sit with my grandson, Max, to watch one of his favorite cartoons, *The Stinky and Dirty Show,* the main characters, a garbage truck and a backhoe, are best friends. They work together to solve problems around their town, and when faced with a challenge ask the question, "What if?" They try several times combining a child's enthusiasm with persistence and creativity each time asking "what if" before they finally fix the dilemma. Two simple words that are powerful. What if? And if we pursue "what if," what's the worst that could happen?

That's the great thing about hanging around a 2-year-old. It is an age of discovery. Everything is new. The theory states that time passes faster when we are in a set routine, when we aren't learning anything new, when we stay stuck in a life pattern. In addition as we get older our frame of reference is larger. So time flies. The key to making time slow down is to have new experiences. Everything is new to a youngster. That is why time slows down in their presence.

And then it was over. Ted described to me how all of a sudden in May of 1945 one day the Germans were no longer there. They were gone. They simply walked away, it was over. As suddenly as it began it ended, as they stood in a field with rakes, recognizing the Nazi's had disappeared. Nowhere to be seen. New journeys would be ahead leading to a long life where now at the age of 104 we sit together talking. And in his journey, just like the comrade with the POW farm labor idea, people had been placed in his path to set the road straight. Now I'm in his path ... providentially placed?

Tinder, spark, breeze. Sometimes the right person is in the right spot at the right time. And through a providential combination of design and a dash of luck you're back on your way and wiser to boot. It's almost as though life requires you to adjust your cadence. The tinder is your mind and heart. The spark is provided by the person in your path. The breeze of new thought fans the flames of your passions moving forward.

Some are just trying to navigate the path. Others are seeking something better, the quest for the ideal. I think about how many are in a quest for the ideal in their lives. The dirty little secret is we really don't want to achieve the ideal. The mystery and the pursuit IS the reward of our journey. We learn more from our mistakes and failures than our successes. We just have to own them.

Wisdom is knowing the right thing to do and doing it at the right time to get the desired result.

If controlling people are on one side of life's pendulum and passive victims on the other, then life should be somewhere in the adventurous middle. If we aren't befuddled, our journey has not yet begun. But that's the fascinating reality. The adventure isn't on the extreme ends. It's in the middle, your chosen path. You have to own your narrative and then share it to love your neighbor as yourself. Well that, in some cases, is a difficult if not impossible goal if you're honest with your human frailties. Maybe we'll start with you being the one who is in the path of someone and nudges their directional compass. One step at a time. Maybe you won't even realize you did it. If Ted's theory is correct, a higher being, a higher purpose, put you in the right place at the right time for someone else. And if you're not willing to own your story then shame owns you, discredits you. If you don't own your story, mistakes and all, then an element of shame owns you. Makes you a passive victim. You never saw the person or opportunity set in your path. Maybe because you wanted total control. Maybe you wanted to be a passive victim. The adventure is in the mystery and pursuit along the path of life. And it happens in the middle ... your path.

Everyone has a narrative. It's up to you to interpret it. That's why telling stories is so important. There is enough conflict, animosity and struggle between opposing sides or beliefs in this world. People pick a side, entrench, and a stalemate struggle ensues. Many times over the course of history we have seen that struggle result in disaster. When people share stories, however, it draws us closer with the realization we have emotions and thoughts in common. We all have more in common than we think. Stories can break a log jam and make us more human.

It's just like the fungi on a log on the path. You can be that person in someone's path. Be a bright spot in a dark place. Many fungi have bioluminescent tendencies and stand out in the dark of the woods. Not only "fun-guys" they have radiant personalities. Not "mushroom" for improvement there! The analogy for me when I walk through a hollow and see their luminescence is how "fun-guys" can light up a dark place just by their presence. Nature always teaches us a lesson. If a hollow is a depressed or low area, then we need more "fun-guys" that deliver the bioluminescence.

In the spring of 2020 I could no longer visit with Ted Szczepanski. Due to lock down and stay at home orders a worldwide pandemic was particularly hard on nursing home residents. What I feared came to pass when his son messaged me that Dad was sick and getting tested. He tested positive for Covid-19. But Ted beat Covid-19 at the age of 104. Add it to accomplishments in his journey along the path.

- World War II veteran, 95th Division Infantry
- Prisoner of war for 6 months in France
- Father of 3 kids

- Devoted husband to Mary who met the suffering of multiple sclerosis with a positive attitude.
- Successful Businessman (with his brother Harry)
- Beat pneumonia 3 times over the age of 100
- Battled Covid-19 diagnosis at the age of 104 and beat it.

Ted taught me the journey is never a straight line. It moves forward from side to side in a zigzag motion. Your attitude and recognition of others along the path can take some of the zig out of your zag and some zag out of your zig. Proceed in faith with a positive attitude.

Beach School

Another "Oakley" in my life was my friend, Ed DeBruyn. Ed taught me how to water ski. He would start any new skier with a process he called "beach school." Through the years he taught many aspiring skiers by showing them what to do with a simple rope and patience. With two skis on your feet in the bindings you would plant your back side on the back of skis along the shoreline. Ed would take a rope and be the boat. Pulling on the rope the skis would slide on the wet sand giving you the sensation of a pull from the boat. You would use the tension to lift into an upright position eventually standing on the skis.

It gave you an element of confidence as you eventually found yourself bobbing in the water on your back, with two skis wobbling tips moving around in front of you. As the boat kicks into gear and the slack comes out of the rope the tension stiffens the skis on your legs and beach school practice pays off. The roar of the boat and the forward progress causes you to stand on the skis until you are in an upright position skimming the water's surface. He had shown you what to do. Now you were going to experience it. Once you had mastered the function of starting on two skis, cutting in and out of the wake, and release and approach on reentry to the beach area with a smooth landing, Ed was quick to present you with a new challenge. He did this so your cocky confidence could be dropped a few pegs. After some trips around the lake on two skis you become dangerous. *This isn't so hard* you think to yourself.

Your presumptuous position on slabs of wood skimming the lake at over 30 miles per hour is about to become bumptious in a hurry. That happens when you eventually are told to drop a ski and wallow along on one slalom ski while awkwardly trying to find a home for your suddenly bare foot due to the vacated ski. As you attempt to secure your foot into the back of the slalom ski the board fishtails and you fight for control. The end result is usually a less-than-graceful face plant in the water with progress coming to an abrupt halt. You bob to the surface, reorient and swim to the errant ski. The boat circles around with the rope and you suddenly realize you don't have two foundational skis to get back out of the water. Things have changed since beach school. Welcome to the world of the deepwater start. Trying to stand up too early is one of the most common mistakes on deepwater starts. Before you can stand on the water, the ski must pivot at your feet and become parallel with the water level. This requires the proper amount of forward speed, and, if you try to stand before you've reached that speed, your ski will plow heavily through the water, resulting in a failed or thoroughly exhausting attempt. The boat is moving forward whether you're coming along or not. Many skiers will over-correct and try to hurry the process, but inevitably the boat is what will pull you out of the water, so until it has reached speed your job is simply to hang in there. Some strength, a lot of persistence and patience get you there. You have to get the ski transitioned from 90 degrees to parallel with the water level, and, once parallel, stabilized with your weight back. But Ed knew I would have to learn by experience. I'm in the water with one ski, knowing I would have to plow water before speed and timing would get me on top of the water. I can still picture Ed in the boat with about 75 foot of rope between me and him. Wearing his Navy baseball cap and aviator sunglasses he glanced into the boat's rearview mirror and hollered his simple instruction. "Follow the boat."

One of the most important lessons I learned from Ed DeBruyn was this:

"A good man doesn't tell you how to do it, he shows you."

I learned something about Ed at his funeral that I did not know all the years I knew him. It's why this Bible verse was used at the memorial service for him.

> *"For I know the plans I have for you,"*
> *declares the Lord, "plans to prosper you and*
> *not to harm you, plans to give you hope and*
> *a future."*
> *– Jeremiah 29:11 (NIV)*

Ed served in the Navy on the USS Midway. The USS Midway was the longest-serving aircraft carrier in the 20th century. Named after the climactic Battle of Midway of June 1942, Midway was built in only 17 months, but missed World War II by one week when commissioned on September 10, 1945. You see a big sign in yellow letters on the Midway warning to "beware of jet blast props and rotors." Jet blasts can easily throw a person over the side. Ed learned his lesson the hard way and almost lost his life in the process as a young man. A simple fence snagged him from potential disaster when caught in a jet blast. A man of faith and principled, I think that experience was one of many that grounded him and molded him into the example he was for other men. He exhibited patience, measured his words and led by example. **Example as in not telling you how, but showing you how.** It has a bigger impact than words. Ed was an Oakley in my path with lessons learned which I now use everyday.

I learned from the examples of Oakleys who went before me that those who were able to ***combine strength with empathy*** were the best leaders. Whether you believe it or not, my life lesson and example that I want to apply for the balance of my life is this equation: ***Strength + Empathy = Leader.*** And true leaders know how to exhibit and provide a measure of grace.

Never stop learning

Another Oakley is my friend, Professor Bill. I call him the professor because he never stops learning. Bill Oomkes will call me out of the blue with an observation, a thought or a question. And he and I are the only people I know who carry a soil thermometer in our vehicles. Used at a moment's notice while out and about measuring soil temperature. On a March day my phone will ring and I'll see it's Bill calling.

"Hi Bill"

"Yep. Soil temperature is 40 degrees at the 2-inch level. I think winter is over."

"Nowhere to go but up from here."

"Yep. Just thought you might want to know. Have a good day."

Bill knows I'm capable of measuring soil temperature myself and can access the data online. But he calls because he knows we are both curious and it's a bond of brothers. I supposed it was good company as intelligent people have a distinguishing characteristic; they are insatiably curious. Albert Einstein was considered by many to be the smartest person in history. He would say, "I have no special talents. I am only passionately curious."

Bill also calls because he knows how much I dislike winter and cold weather. He even hesitates to express that four-letter word around me called snow. Bill combines his curiosity and questions with a positive attitude. As kids we are encouraged to ask questions and are rewarded for learning. As adults questioning often comes with negative connotations. It shouldn't. We are continually learning to the day we die. Bill is always learning and maintains a positive attitude, and that attitude is infectious around others. The combination of curiosity and a positive attitude is a great "Oakley" example for me to follow. Looking forward.

Bill also loves to travel and share his discoveries with others. But with his wife ill and no longer able to travel, the professor too ended up in the hospital during the spring of 2020. Some very serious issues. You wouldn't know it by talking to him. My phone rings on a warm May day.

Bill says, "Why are the forsythias in bloom? It's mid-May."

I have to prod him to talk about his hospital stay and how *he* is doing. He had to be readmitted after an initial stay. He would rather talk about the forsythias blooming late due to a cold ,wet spring; to talk about how pre-emergent applications for crabgrass controls might be affected; how beautiful the blooming trees are. And how blessed we are. Curious and positive. Together we never stop learning.

He did it

One of my ultimate Oakley's is my friend Virgil Westdale. An American WWII hero and 102 years old. A man with more than a lifetime of experiences that included overcoming discrimination and amazing accomplishments including 25 U.S. patents for his work, as well as his heroic service to our country. Virgil, just as I surmise my favorite oak tree along the path, calls the good times "blue skies" and the difficulties "thunder and lightning."

Another example of insatiable curiosity. "I love new thoughts and learning," says Virgil. With a twinkle in his eye he says, "I'm a sucker for it." I sat in a McDonalds with him and asked Virgil, "How did you accomplish what you did in life?" He bows his head and sets his coffee on the table. (Ironically we both got the senior coffee.) He replies by reciting this poem from memory which I now carry in my heart and in my mind.

"Somebody said that it couldn't be done,
But he with a chuckle replied
That "maybe it couldn't," but he would be one
Who wouldn't say so till he'd tried.
So he buckled right in with the trace of a grin
On his face. If he worried he hid it.
He started to sing as he tackled the thing
That couldn't be done, and he did it."

Virgil, who loves swing dancing, has been on the "dance floor" his entire life and is another example of curiosity and a positive attitude. Virgil accomplished so much in his lifetime. And yet he demonstrated to me that it's not always what you ***did*** in life, but it's what you ***didn't do*** that will create regret later in life. In the case of Virgil he lived life to the fullest as a great example to others. He fell and broke his hip the summer of 2020. I couldn't visit him due to Covid 19 and restrictions at the home where he lives. But if anyone could tackle a thing like a pandemic and a broken hip it would be Virgil. He would *buckle right in with a trace of a grin*.

What I found with Oakleys was this: ***Suffering didn't break or embitter them but rather deepened them.*** Just like that storm-battered oak tree on my path; it enriched them with character and standing. It made them wise. They can balance empathy with reality. We're all on a path, but the key is having a purpose on that path. The example they set for me is they bent but didn't break; they became resolved not embittered, and understood sometimes your purpose is embedded in your pain. Lessons learned. We need those Oakleys in our lives. We need to hear their stories, Oakley's oracles. They need to tell their stories. They can help us discover our purpose on our path by their example. If we listen, their purpose, their resolve, their experience may help us avoid some self-induced pain.

And when does someone become "old" anyhow? If you are 25 and refer to me as a senior citizen do you really want me to call you junior? Some may say 65 is retirement age but it's not "old." 65 might not be old but it's not middle-age either. Do you live by metrics and a script or by a better nature? I prefer the latter, whatever your age. I don't think I'll ever retire. I would feel like a hot dog in a steakhouse. Does old age have to start at a certain time? I'm not old, I'm just older. I'm not elderly I'm "elder." Maybe I can use the natural example set by the Elder tree.

The American elder species, *Sambucus canadensis*, is native to North America with large growth populations occurring east of the Rocky Mountains. It is popular for its dense thicket and versatility. It is said that nearly every part of the tree has a use. Aside from wildlife enjoying the berries, they are also great in baking jams, juice, pies and wine and the flower petals can be used in teas. The tree is one of the oldest plant sources of medicine.

Regardless of the analogy, I want the elder discount instead of the senior discount. And I want to become an "Oakley" and an "Elder" in the time I have left, using the example gifted me by others on the path before me. Then I'm golden.

Through all the human race
We needed to extend some grace
Troubles come in trio
A perplexing imbroglio
When between a rock and hard place.

Chapter Six
Between a Grok and a Hard Place

I WALK DOWN CHURCH STREET IN NEW York City and make the turn on Liberty heading toward West street. I stop, stand still on the sidewalk, and close my eyes. The history seems to permeate the soles of my shoes and fill me with a wistful sadness for the tragic past this pavement has witnessed. I am standing where Radio Row had been the hub of the electronics industry in New York from the 1920s through the 1950s. Radio Row's popularity peaked in the 1950s. Many of the shops would be open by 7AM on weekdays and stay open late on Saturdays to meet the demand, open everyday except Sunday. The neighborhood controversially was leveled in the mid-1960s to make way for the World Trade Center.

Post war demand for consumer electronics and the popularity of radio fueled the intrigue of blocks of family-owned mom and pop electronics shops now gone ... a part of history. I envision the store fronts with signage and slogans. I see Oldsmobile sedans and coupes on the street. I imagine the people walking from shop to shop as fashion in the 1940s was a mix of comfort and glamour. Men wore suits, ties and hats, and the ladies wore dresses, skirts and gloves, commonplace attire in public. I envision the Radio Row merchants and their economic village steeling themselves for the titanic battle against the forces of progress. Battling governments, legislatures, public port authorities and Manhattan financial interests in the early 1960s, they were doomed to fail. Hundreds of businesses employing thousands of people would have to close. The demolitions started on March 26, 1966. Tragically, years later on the morning of September 11, 2001, militant terrorist hijackers associated with the Islamic extremist group al Qaeda flew two commercial airliners into the North and South towers of the World Trade Center, causing both towers to collapse. Close to 3,000 people in and within the vicinity of the towers and all those on board the aircraft lost their lives that day and I pause to remember.

I stand there and imagine some kind of time machine that could take me back to the golden age of radio. A time when cathedral style radios became a central piece of furniture in the home. Everyone would gather around. We would follow the exploits of the Lone Ranger or The Shadow as they work their way out of deadly capers. To laugh along with Jack Benny or Fred Allen. To be comforted in times of trouble and a fireside chat with FDR. To hear an announcer describe the moment the "Great Bambino" would launch another home run and envision the "Sultan of Swat" in pinstripes circling the bases. To receive news on current events from the "talking telegram" such as the colossus Hindenburg tragically exploding in midair and reporter Herb Morrison on the scene painting pictures with words of the calamity.

Radio was the first medium of instant communication to masses of people. Mass opinions were made or swayed, and marketing sponsors were born of this technology. The world would never be the same.

I love radio and have broadcast live shows for close to 30 years. Methods, stations and people have come and gone through the years. If there is one thing we can be assured of it is change. But painting pictures with words through the medium of radio is something that never gets old for me no matter how technology advances. The golden age of radio has come and gone, and I'm something of an outlier fighting not to be "relocated" by advances and change just like the ghosts of radio row I feel around me on Liberty street.

In a crisis we heard the word "outlier" used in conversations and news reports with increased frequency. Those who resisted or bucked the generally accepted principles of collectively dealing with a difficult situation were given this label. An outlier is a thing situated away or detached from the main body or system. In the case of human beings it would be a person who differs or disagrees from everyone in a group. In geology, it would be a feature that lies apart from the main body or mass to which it belongs; maybe a rock formation or stratum of rock that has been separated from a formation by erosion. Some geologists refer to an outlier as an area of younger rock completely surrounded by older rocks which is exactly how I would describe my taste in music compared to my kids. I'm a baby boomer outlier. It seems to me both outliers themselves and the use of the word in 2020 was abundant, because everyone was trying to find footing and an understanding of exactly what the new normal was in a shifting landscape. Once the perceived footing was found they would take a stand. Normal was open to interpretation and outliers from a group consensus stood out from the crowd. For many, they found themselves between a rock and a hard place.

GROK
Understanding intuitively with empathy.

Grok is a terrestrial guttural earthy word that escapes the bonds of singular reality. It is an understanding that goes beyond the facts and applies intuitive sense. In human terms it involves intuitive communication. It's about receiving non-verbal information through all of your senses and perceptions. You do this all the time when you get a feeling or an impression from another person. Some certainly better than others. The theory is, in nature you can do this also with plants. Plant whisperers.

The Dutch have a great word "domp" which means to be dull, down and overturned. Maybe that's where the phrase "down in the dumps" originated. If your hydrangeas have the blues, your geraniums glum and your magnolia is melancholy, your ability to intuitively sense, and your rapport with the plant, just might make you a "plant whisperer." As preposterous as this may seem to some, over time plant people such as myself can spot a wilting plant in trouble from a long distance away. Its present state and posture, color and characteristics are recognizable from afar, calling out for supplemental help beyond what nature can currently provide. It is why some recommend that a youngster first own some plants before owning a pet; it develops some nurturing sense for other living things. The analogy has a measure of reason that those with a developed sense to identify a wilting Weigela from a distance may also have the ability to see that you too aren't having the best of days.

Between a Grok and a hard place

Throughout my life I've learned that progress is expeditious when times are challenging and difficult. I have learned to be effective when working with resolve while simultaneously applying a measured dose of empathy in the process. It's the "we're in this together" sentiment that people tire of hearing. Instead of saying the words, show others through your actions. When you hit an unexpected reality you have to adjust quickly. Life comes at you fast. Some are better able to do this than others. During the 2008 financial crisis the accumulation of unregulated derivatives and complicated financial products, including mortgage-backed securities rapidly lost their value, and the economy for all of us quickly tanked. Businesses and their people had to adjust rapidly. When things change in a matter of days you find yourself between a rock and a hard place.

Weed need to talk

Why is it that weeds pop up where you least expect them? Why does grass grow best where we don't want it? Grass and weeds growing out of pavement cracks in sidewalks, driveways, and parking areas seem to adjust and flourish in a hard place. Weeds and grass seem to grow best in the cracks and crevices of driveways and sidewalks, which defies logic, because these are hot unforgiving places to survive. Not only do they survive they seem to thrive.

You would be surprised at the amount of organic matter and soil that collects in the expansion joints and cracks of pavement. It's nice and warm for seeds to settle and stabilize then grow. And moisture that seeps into driveway and sidewalk cracks remains a lot longer than in other parts of the landscape. Water runs down the impermeable surface finding its way to the cracks. The driveway then holds moisture beneath the surface, much the same way mulch does, and any plant that sends its roots down below the slab has access to this trapped moisture. And when the going gets tough, many grasses and weeds, like crabgrass, thrive in the heat.

An annual grass, like crabgrass, produces thousands of seeds, and can opportunistically acclimatize in the smallest of openings. Perennial grasses like quackgrass only need a small portion of their rhizomatous root to remain and continue to remind you they are there for the long haul. If the exposed portion of the grass is removed, a new shoot will pop up in no time at all.

Problems often crop up when and where you least expect

them, often on the margins like those weeds in the cracks. In most cases you didn't see them coming. Many for years have argued the nature vs. nurture theory. Do we react to a crisis because we are trained by societal influences or because it's simply how we were individually raised and wired? Is your reaction natural or nurtured?

The middle ground is not always a bad place. It often is where common sense dwells. Common ground. Especially if you can mentally handle two opposing views and still continue to function.

In the spring of 2020 there was a significant economic impact due to the infectious pandemic that swept up everyone in its path. It took businesses well on their way to a successful year, in a strong economy, and in a matter of weeks took them from "shoot for the moon" to survival mode. I found it ironic this all happened during the observation of the 50th anniversary of the Apollo 13 mission in April of 1970. Dubbed a "successful failure" the anticipated moon landing instantly on the evening of April 13, 2020, became a mission of survival with a simple cryo stir of an oxygen tank, 200,000 miles from earth. Houston we've had a problem. A move from Odyssey to Aquarius and a herculean effort on the part of many ensued in the following days to creatively solve a big problem. Shoot for the moon became instead a laser focus on survival. The agenda in a world of endless options suddenly changed to failure is ***not*** an option. It's amazing what can be done when you're between a rock and a hard place.

> *"Only when the tide goes out do you discover who's been swimming naked."*
> *– Warren Buffett*

We as businesses had launched 2020 with high hopes and a strong economy. We had talked and kept in the back of our minds a possible impending "course correction" or softening downturn after a long robust bull market economy. Nothing prepared us for what the coronavirus caused in a matter of weeks. A world of options for many entrepreneurial businesses quickly turned into "failure is not an option" survival mode. We moved from a possible course correction of years of robust growth to a Thelma and Louise moment, staring at an approaching cliff. No longer concerned with ***corrections,*** it became an issue of ***continuance.*** You have to do something. When nothing is going right, turn left and hang on.

Some people debate whether he ever said it, but the performer Will Rogers is credited with the quote, "I am more concerned with the return **of** my money than return **on** my money." It doesn't matter if he ever said it, close to a century after the height of his popularity, its meaning rang true. It was to circle the wagons and batten the hatches as we figured this out.

Will Rogers life ended abruptly and tragically August 15, 1935 at Point Barrow in the Alaska Territory due to a plane crash. It is said an Eskimo, who moments before had given Rogers and the aviator Wiley Post directions to Point Barrow in foggy conditions, witnessed the crash. He in turn ran the 15 miles to Point Barrow for help. He ran the distance in 3 hours. Those were 12-minute miles, which is amazing considering he did not have the running gear we have today and was done over rough tundra with streams to cross and lakes to circle. You do what you have to do. And you will be amazed what you are capable of if needed. Real-life experiences have prepared you for the moment.

> Some people are wired in crisis to see opportunity. Don't waste a crisis. Trade drama for introspective dedication.

A Hardening Off

So when plants are pampered in a greenhouse setting, and then suddenly thrust into the real world, the results can be devastating. Plants, like people, can become soft, and need a hardening off before planted in the real earth for what lies ahead. Wind, sun, cold, heat, and stresses. True character of both plants and people are sure to be revealed in less than pampered or shall we say stressful environments.

Crisis reveals character. Some rise to the occasion despite seemingly insurmountable odds. I think in the years preceding a crisis the individual is "hardened off" by life experiences and cashes them in when faced with their Waterloo. Unlike Napoleon and his troops in the Battle of Waterloo, you can prevail victorious in a crisis. It's the getting there part that is so hard. I can't imagine the strain on someone like Abraham Lincoln in the final 4 years of his life. While hated by some at the time and threatened with death by opponents, Lincoln stood tall and in his March 1861 inaugural address said:

> **I need to change my plants:** When you quit but keep going, you're going through the motions and drag everyone else down with you. If you quit, start over. Failure is only the end if you give up. A failure is an opportunity for a new beginning.

> *"The mystic chords of memory, stretching from every battlefield and patriot grave to every living heart and hearthstone all over this broad land, will yet swell the chorus of the Union, when again touched, as surely they will be, by the better angels of our nature."*

A true leader, Lincoln set the example that in difficult situations leaders are able to couple strength with empathy. They also humble themselves and lower their position to unite in the common interest of defeating a common foe. Not just express sentiments but truly demonstrate the better of angels of our nature.

> *"As a man changes his own nature, so does the attitude of the world change towards him."*
>
> *– Mahatma Ghandi*

I Just Wet My Plants

Maybe it's not a crisis but rather a drought, a dry spell, a period of unsuccessful attempts. In nature if you've gone through a dry patch, a drought, the anticipation of rain is rejuvenating. And if you love the smell of rain when it hits dry dirt, the experience is amplified with the sensory pleasure. For most our olfactory receptors pick up and embrace that unique aroma. A mixture of fresh air and damp soil that has a name: Petrichor. Researchers believe that bacteria resting dormant in the soil releases tiny microbes into the air when they get doused with rainwater. During a springtime shower or summer thunderstorm, the air becomes perfumed with the fragrant molecules, causing petrichor. Bacteria, plants and even lightning can all play a role in the pleasant smell of clean air and wet earth. What you are smelling is a molecule, geosmin, made by a bacteria in healthy soils called streptomyces. Many antibiotics used today are made by a group of bacteria called streptomyces.

I Need to Change My Plants

It turns out it's not just gratitude that makes rain smell so appealing after a long period of dry weather.

When raindrops hit the ground it causes geosmin to be released into the air, making a walk after a storm a therapeutic nasal event. The word was coined from Greek *petros*, meaning "stone", and *ichor*, meaning "the fluid that flows in the veins of the gods." It just smells like gratitude.

A dirty little secret

Statistics have suggested that the average Dad spends up to 7 hours a year in the bathroom simply hiding from the family. The lawn was always the man's domain, but women can cut the grass as well if not better than a man. The dirty little secret is Dad likes to mow the lawn, because the drone is mindless and an escape and that's why Mom wants to do it too.

Solitude is sometimes stigmatized with a label of "loners." When we all had to distance during a pandemic we found once again the garden, a wooded walk, the nurture of plants was therapeutic. Sure we all need community, but we also need solitude from time to time. We just don't want it forced on us. And during that time of solitude in the garden, we gain an understanding and acceptance of *you don't know what you don't know*. It's a realization of how much we don't know. And that's OK. Instead of frustration, it's an opportunity to learn, an opportunity to grow.

"I work like a gardener," the famous Spanish painter and sculptor Joan Miró wrote in his meditation on establishing a proper pace for your work. "Things come slowly ... things follow their natural course." *Well Miro never watched me work,* I thought. As a homeowner when you get home from work at night and have only a couple hours before dark, you learn to plant, mow, fertilize and trim at a frenetic pace. Forget supper; there is weeding to do; plants to water; flowers to put in the ground; edging to set. Your work is never done, and you are up against the clock. The life of a working, homeowning father who wants a nice yard. Plants maintain their pace however, namely perennials and woody plants like shrubs, evergreens and trees no matter how quickly I work. They have a biological clock that works at their pace. Gardeners have noted this in the form of a mnemonic that notes they "sleep, creep and leap."

Mnemonics is an auditory aid that helps an individual remember something. Mnemonics can come in different forms including acronyms. As a Michigander we were taught "HOMES" to remember the Great Lakes: Huron, Ontario, Michigan, Erie, and Superior. As a horticulturist I was taught to remember the order of Taxonomy: kingdom, phylum, class, order, family, genus, species as "Kids prefer cheese over fried green spinach." Or when I string and tune my guitar starting from the thickest, lowest-pitched string (the 6th string) at the top of neck E A D G B E using the mnemonics "Eddie ate dynamite good bye Eddie. Or if I tuned from the thinnest highest pitched 1st string EBGDAE is "Easter bunnies get dizzy at Easter." It just makes progressions easier to remember.

I enjoy creating acronyms but mnemonic poems can also stay with you throughout life. Especially the ones you were taught as a kid. Poems like, Red sky at night, Shepherd's delight, Red sky in the morning shepherds warning. My Dad taught it to me as Red sky at night, sailors' delight. Red sky in morning, sailors' warning. Since then I've always loved a sunset sky bathed in red, and am wary of an eastern red sky in the morning.

Leap Year

Gardeners have a mnemonic that proves to be true in the landscape and that is "sleep, creep, leap". Nature has its course and instant gratification is not one of them. If you're a gardener, it is best to cultivate patience when dealing with woody plants, trees, perennials and "long-term" plants. Expect that its first year will be one of little apparent growth. In other words it "sleeps." Hopefully the work is happening out of sight or underground as the root system works to establish the plant. One year later it is said that the plant "creeps."

During the sleep and creep stage, for Type-A-personality gardeners the space between plants in the planted landscape presentation is wide and yawning and progress is painstakingly slow. Finally in the third, fourth or fifth year, the plants begin to fill their appointed space and look like a full garden. During the initial planting or in the sleep and creep years; they are lured into the pitfall of over-planting to fill the uncomfortable space and methodical pace. To achieve the illusion of an "instant garden," the spacing recommendations for maturity are ignored and the space is filled. It's like those who are bothered by uncomfortable moments of silence in a conversation, and they try to fill the space instead of letting it breathe a little bit. By the third "leap" year, plants are getting in one another's way. By the fifth year, shrubs that ought to be thriving and putting on a show are crowded, unhappy and in some cases showing you their vexation. Your pace didn't match theirs and even though you think you're in charge nature will show you its opinion via vegetation vexation. I see it all the time.

Sometimes it's good to slow down. Gain perspective in the process. There is a pace that I don't think I've ever learned. It doesn't always have to be fast. An Eephus pitch is very slow and is used to catch the batter off guard. The pitch was invented by Rip Sewell of the Pittsburgh Pirates in the 1940s. The name Eephus pitch comes from the Hebrew word *efes*, which means "nothing." A reminder that slow can sometimes be good. Not everything has to be rapid. It's like a dopamine fast. It's not always cliche to stop and smell the roses.

Kinesthetic people like me want to see everyone including themselves moving all the time. It's not that they are not thoughtful, they just do their best thinking when mowing the lawn, running, working. Vines tend to be kinesthetic characteristically. Always moving and growing. But an event, a stress, a change can stop them in their tracks and get them to refocus and bloom. A root pruning can get them to stop the incessant setting of tendrils in search of constant growth to instead do some flowering.

Talking to your plants

Talking to ourselves is completely within the norm in my opinion. Most of us talk to ourselves on a daily basis. Talking to your plants may only benefit them by the volume of carbon dioxide you are spewing from your mouth. They in turn will gift you with oxygen. I like talking to plants because it benefits me. In any situation or task when we talk to ourselves, it slows us down and helps us process our behavior. When dealing with a crisis or difficult situation, if we're talking to ourselves negatively, we're more likely to engage in negative behavior. When our self talk is neutral, as in a statement like "What do I need to do?" we slow down and reason our way through it more effectively. If your self talk is positive, like "I've got this" then the outcome is more effective, efficient and successful. When between a rock and hard place do yourself a favor and talk to yourself. You'll feel much better.

My friend Quercus

In addition to learning from the Oakleys in my life, I benefit from conversations with my imaginary friend Quercus. These conversations are helpful when facing a quandary or if between a rock and a hard place. Quercus is a good listener. Ridiculous you say? I think everyone should have an imaginary friend to whom they can air their thoughts out. It's not much different than a Nom de Plume, a name that a writer uses instead of his or her real name. I use the pseudonym Quercus to air out my thoughts in a risk-free environment.

I Need to Change My Plants

Between October 1787 and May 1788 as an example, The *Federalist Papers* were written and published to persuade New Yorkers to ratify the proposed United States Constitution, drafted in Philadelphia in the summer of 1787. The papers, a series of 85 essays, were written by Alexander Hamilton, John Jay, and James Madison. The essays were published anonymously, under the pen name "Publius," in various New York state newspapers of the time. Hamilton chose Publius as the pseudonym under which the *Federalist Papers* would be written, in honor of the great Roman Publius Valerius Publicola. The original Publius is credited with being instrumental in the founding of the Roman Republic. Publius, meaning public or friend of the people, along with three other Romans, led a successful rebellion against the king of Rome, and the formation of the Roman Republic. Publius and his efforts for liberty inspired the authors of the *Federalist Papers*, namely Hamilton, to write under a pseudonym of the same name. The papers aired the thoughts in the form of a letter to the people of New York. It became a foundation for the federal system of democratic government that the United States has today.

Airing out your thoughts whether in a conversation to yourself or others is beneficial to sorting out your way forward. I'm told the average person will make 773,618 decisions over a lifetime and will come to regret 143,262 of them. Seems hard to believe and I regret reading that statistic, Yet good things can happen when you move with purpose and a willingness to make some mistakes. Let's give others the grace to make some mistakes. You can't possibly live long enough to make all of them yourself. And if you're struggling with that concept, ask your own inner Quercus. He'll know what to do when between a rock and a hard place.

Rick Vuyst

What happened not a mystery
Involved the humble lavatory
The troubles were antecedent
And not without a precedent
Its past was rooted in history

Chapter Seven
Quintessential Normalcy

I LIKE TO SAY THAT MUCH OF WHAT WE worry about is rooted in historical precedent. We don't need a crystal ball ... we need to understand history. 2020 wasn't the first time we feared shortages. It made me think of the hoarding and stockpiling of rations like canned goods, water and even cash prior to Y2K in 1999. It was fear of a digital pandemic as the world's calendar moved to the year 2000. A number of people thought it was the end of the world as we knew it. We had never entered a new millennium with computers in control of societal functions. Fear of the Y2K millennium bug as we turned forward to 2000 created a blip of anxious preparation on the part of some people. Those who feared it and prepared for it drove those who didn't nuts. As Y2K became a part of the mainstream lexicon in the late 1990s there was some hoarding and stories of some going to the point of building nuclear fallout safe spaces in the backyard. If banks, nuclear power stations, the electrical grid and computer systems failed it would be all-out chaos. That never materialized. We celebrated New Years day and everyone went back to work groggy and relieved on January 2.

I Need to Change My Plants

If you look to the past (study history) there are answers for how to react in the present.

The run on toilet paper in 2020 was not without historical precedent. Toilet paper was wiped out on store shelves in short order in March of that year. In today's digital-age, word got around rapidly that you'd better stock up. Everybody likes to be the first to know something. In the old days, a rumor took a long time to spread, enough time to let people vet and challenge its validity. The fear of missing out drives people to act. Americans had cultivated a "shortage psychology" in the midst of crisis. But for historical precedent all you needed to do was go back to 1973 to understand why.

The economic recession in 1973 came about because of rocketing gas prices caused by the Organization of the Petroleum Exporting Countries (OPEC) raising oil prices and embargoing oil exports to the United States. Between January of 1973 and December of 1974 the New York Stock Exchange Dow Jones Industrial Average benchmark lost about 45% of its value in a bear market. There was heavy government spending due to the Vietnam War, with President Nixon signing the Paris Peace Accords, ending direct U.S. involvement in the Vietnam War in 1973. Inflation, recession, unemployment, an energy crisis, Nixon's resignation and questions of financial stability rocked the economy. The U.S. spiraled into a period of economic stagnation and malaise it hadn't seen since the Great Depression.

For most Americans, 1973 was marred by shortages. Gasoline, electricity, and onions of all things were reported as goods and services that were in limited supply. Onions? Now this was a problem of Biblical proportions. Again rooted in history we go way back and read:

> *"We remember the fish we ate in Egypt at no cost—also the cucumbers, melons, leeks, onions and garlic."*
>
> *– Numbers 11:5 (NIV)*

In 1973 many of the onions had rotted before they ripened, victims of flooding in the Texas onion belt where much of the American crop is grown. The onion had become a costly status symbol that year. If you wanted onion rings or French onion soup it was a luxury that only the very affluent or the desperate could buy.

Then came a toilet paper fiasco in 1973, and it all started with an unsubstantiated rumor. Someone said something and fear of missing out caused people to act. Actually it was a congressman and a famous comedian that started the befuddled dither over the bathroom essential.

There were rumors in November 1973 of a reported tissue shortage in Japan. A U.S. congressman Harold Froelich of Wisconsin took notice. He presided over a heavily-forested district in Wisconsin, and had recently been receiving complaints from constituents about a reduced stream of pulp paper. To make pulp and paper you need fiber. Paper fiber comes mainly from three sources: by-products from the sawmilling process, pulpwood logs and recycled paper products. Much of the paper we use every day is a blend of new and recycled fiber. Waste from log cutting that is left over is converted to wood chips or "corn flakes." The chips are then put in pulp digesters and broken down into a gloppy pudding of cellulose fibers. I always figured a mechanical process was used and the wood chips were literally beaten to a pulp. Regardless of the process, if the components are in short supply you can't make paper. And congressman Froelich was following a paper trail of evidence to uncover the impending crisis.

I Need to Change My Plants

Froelich had uncovered a document that indicated the government's National Buying Center had fallen far short of securing bids to provide toilet paper for its troops and bureaucrats. On December 11, 1973 he issued this ominous press release:

> *"The U.S. may face a serious shortage of toilet paper within a few months...we hope we don't have to ration toilet tissue...a toilet paper shortage is no laughing matter. It is a problem that will potentially touch every American."*

In the climate of shortages, oil scares, and economic duress, Froelich's claim was accepted as truth without vetting and the media ran with the story. The words "may" and "potentially" were dropped and the story was sensationalized. The kindling had been placed for a consumer panic; all it needed was a spark to ignite it.

Tinder, spark, breeze. Enter television host and comedian Johnny Carson. Ironically Carson himself would, a few years later, be involved in lavatory litigation and a company that wanted to use his trademark "Here's Johnny" phrase for a line of portable toilets they sold. The potty proceedings went to the U.S. District Court where the company was told they could not use the phrase. Johnny Carson had sued to stop the practice. He felt he had a right of publicity in that phrase, and the courts agreed after a legal fight that spanned a decade and two appeals in Carson v. Here's Johnny Portable Toilets, Inc.

But when Johnny Carson cracked a joke about toilet paper on his television talk show on December 19, 1973 things got a little out of hand. Millions of viewers were watching when he said,

"You know, we've got all sorts of shortages these days, but have you heard the latest? I'm not kidding. I saw it in the papers. There's a shortage of toilet paper!"

Today in the "on demand" age we live in all it takes is someone with a phone, a social media post and some shares. Years ago news would be slower with much via word of mouth. But in the 1970s it was Johnny Carson and the *Tonight Show* with its millions of viewers about to go to bed. The potty provocateur had lit the shortage psychology of Americans, and all it took was one TV personality to joke about it.

Irrational absurdity ensued and the race to hoard rolls began. Millions of Americans swarmed grocery outlets and hoarded all the toilet paper they could get their hands on. A tussle over tissue. Paper and grocery industry leaders asked the public to remain calm. The price went up and many stores set limits of two rolls per customer.

For months, toilet paper was a rare commodity. Store owners had to "crack down" and limit purchases to clamoring customers. A black market, bartering, trading, even gifting rolls that holiday season ensued. By February of 1974 the calamity subsided as Americans realized that there never had been a shortage in the first place. The shortage myth had finally been tamped down. The story beaten to a pulp finally subsided.

Carnac the Magnificent, better known as Johnny Carson, faced the cameras and apologetically offered a bathroom tissue mea culpa. "I don't want to be remembered as the man who created a false toilet paper scare," he told viewers, "I just picked up the item from the newspaper and enlarged it somewhat ... there is no shortage."

In 1973 as well as the year 2020 it was a good reminder that people used the woodlands, the prairies and were inventive long before toilet paper was invented. Colonial Americans used the core center cobs from shelled ears of corn. Long ago the wealthy used wool and rosewater and others used a sponge attached to a wooden stick, soaked in a bucket of salt water. Eskimos used moss and snow. The French of course not to be out done invented the bidet. The name is rooted in the French word for "pony," which offers a helpful hint that the basin should be straddled. In Old French, bidet meant "to trot." The etymology comes from, yes you guessed it, one who "rides" or straddles a bidet like a pony is ridden. The "pony" was usually kept in the bedroom or dressing chamber and looked like an ottoman. The basin was inset in wood furniture with a lid. A deceptive covering concealing its function. By the 1700s they could include a water pump handle that could deliver an upward spray from a refillable tank. The art and practice of indoor plumbing took nearly a century to develop, starting in the mid 1800s, and, with it the bidet was a luxury of high society. I'm sure you had to pony up plenty of French francs to have one of those in your home.

The bottom line is, as with anything, only some could afford luxurious lavatory solutions. Therein prior to the invention of toilet paper for comfort and absorbance, some of nature's foliage works best in the woodland's wild. It's obvious to steer clear of tree bark, poison ivy, or anything with thorns. You would think common sense would prevail. If the store shelves are wiped out of bath tissue, in a pinch, here are my 8 best natural, as in botanical, options when the store shelves are empty.

Giant Mullein. Cowboy toilet paper. This has to be the obvious choice with thick large fluffy leaves. Cowboys would use this biennial plant out on the range. The range which of course was home. Difficult to miss, the plant grows 4 to 6 feet tall. Like major toilet paper brands it touts the fact it is soft and absorbent.

Stachys byzantina also known as Lambs Ear. Soft, silvery, thick and velvet leaves, if this is at your disposal a fine choice for woolly comfort. Found in every region of the U.S. it is medicinal and super absorbent!

Common Mallow or Malva neglecta also known as marshmallow weed. Soft leaves that are durable and resistant to tear.

Large Leaf Aster Eurybia macrophylla known as Lumberjack toilet paper. Found throughout the Great Lakes region in woodland areas.

Catalpa Heart shaped leaves. So many leaves on one tree you can hoard these as they stack on top of each other. A compound in the leaves has herbal anti-inflammatory properties.

Southern Magnolia Thick, very resistant to tearing with a large surface area. The underside of the leaf is a rust-colored felt.

Broadleaf Plantain A weed often found in lawns with soil compaction or clay; it is plentiful.

Big Leaf Maple *Acer macrophyllum* If you live in the great northwest you're in luck. Think "macro" big and "phyllum" leaf. The bottom line is the rest is up to you.

Quintessential Normalcy

The word essential in the dictionary includes, as part of the definition, the phrase "being such by its very nature or in the highest sense; natural; spontaneous" such as essential happiness. It causes me to think that quintessential then represents the most perfect or typical example of what is *naturally* essential. The definitions are the basis for debate that developed in 2020 due to the pandemic crisis on whether or not greenhouses or garden centers, plants and gardening should be considered "essential" activities. In some states in the US they were deemed essential, in other states they were not. When elected representatives asked me my opinion during the crisis it was easy. I consider hands in the dirt and plants to be natural, essential and even quintessential. After the initial shock of stay-at-home orders, and in the subsequent months that followed, this theory proved to be true. Plants and dirt felt normal. As the world was experiencing upheaval, interaction with plants and the company of plants provided grounding. They became an essential element of coping with a difficult situation.

> Define what is essential
> And that you find inconsequential
> When things are abnormal
> They can get quite informal
> And knowledge becomes inferential

In the midst of a pandemic the word *normalcy* surfaced as a repeatedly used word. The return to normalcy. The first reaction for many based on web searches was, is that really a word? Don't you mean normality?

Ironically the interest in normalcy as a word came exactly one century to the year from the 1920 presidential campaign of Warren G. Harding, who made "The return to normalcy" his central slogan. The American public was war weary after World War I and had just emerged from the deadly 1918 influenza pandemic. Already cast as a less than eloquent orator, Harding was questioned for his use of the word and roundly mocked for its use. In a speech Harding said, "It is time to hark back to sanity and normalcy." In that same speech he doubled down and floated the phrase "the new normalcy." His most famous use of the word came on May 14 of that year, when he delivered an address to the Home Market Club of Boston, stating alliteratively, "America's present need is not heroics, but healing; not nostrums, but normalcy; not revolution, but restoration."

With the Republican nomination in hand by July he seemed to find his footing using "normalcy" as a basis for his message. "I have noticed that word caused considerable newspaper editors to change it to 'normality,'" he said defiantly. Harding had been accused of fabricating the word. "I have looked for 'normality' in my dictionary and I do not find it there. 'Normalcy,' however, I find, and it is a good word."

In tumultuous times the word normalcy resonated with the general populous and helped carry him to victory. In his inaugural address he put an exclamation point on the phrase that won him the White House saying "We must strive for normalcy to reach stability." Our communal lexicon was forever changed with the word only to find renewed popularity 100 years later in the throes of a nationwide pandemic. Now popular after a national crisis, the word has attained a new normalcy.

A tough row to hoe

I've heard pundits and broadcasters mess up the idiom as "we have a tough *road* to hoe." Really? That asphalt has to be tough to cultivate with a hoe, and be careful you're liable to get hit. Maybe because I am a gardener I am attuned to this phrasing faux pas that grinds my gravel.

In farming and gardening, to hoe a row is to turn a line of soil for the planting of seeds or bulbs. The idiom is meant to describe a large, challenging task. A literal tough row to hoe might be one that is long or that involves hoeing dirt with lots of rocks or roots. A figurative tough row to hoe is any large undertaking that is especially difficult. I think that is why I like daylilies so much. I'll take my lesson from the daylilies. They have a tough row to hoe in their prime during summer stress. They stand up to heat and drought with a good attitude. Even though each flower lasts only a day, they make the very most of it and do it with style. One day at a time when facing a challenging task.

Pedal Power

Most people still can't figure out "why a run on toilet paper in the midst of a national and international crisis?" It took months before order was restored to store shelves. I can however understand the run on bicycles, because as far back as the late 1800s bikes were a symbol of freedom. Bike styles developed during the mid to late 1800s with something people called two-wheeled machines, dandy horse, running machine, velocipede or Penny Farthing. Penny Farthing because the wheels resembled two coins, the penny and the farthing next to each other. The front wheel was huge and the seat high in the air. More like a circus act than an exercise ... all done without a net. Extremely difficult and dangerous to get on and off, the front wheel was used for both pedal power and steering. It wasn't until around the mid 1880s that things became a little more comfortable with two wheels of the same size. The bicycle now had a center of gravity and rear wheel connected and driven by a chain. It was much more efficient and practical. It set off a bike craze in both Europe and the United States. It was a New York Times article in 1896 that eloquently explained the interest in bikes for both then and now applicable to 2020 in the midst of a pandemic:

> *"The bicycle promises a splendid extension*
> *of personal power and freedom, scarcely*
> *inferior to what wings would give."*
> *– New York Times 1896*

Whether it is 1896 or 2020 the principle remains the same: supply and demand. A tightening supply goes hand in hand with demand and no one wants to miss out. With ***abnormal*** demands on certain commodities I developed an acronym GAM in my mind trying to explain the elements of a successful service venture.

GAM

If you want a successful organization that serves others you:

Give them what they want

A*dd* what they need

M*ake* an emotional connection.

Drop the microphone

It's not a game it's a "GAM." To create abnormal demand for a product or a service you need to **find** what they *want*, **identify** what they *need* and **focus** on how they *feel*. Then exit stage left. If it was easy everyone would be successful.

Of Chart Datum, Dragonflies and Damselflies

Dragonflies are one of the symbols of summer. With fluttering and graceful flight the large insect draws attention along a lake, stream or pond areas. The bright, almost neon color with shimmering cellophane transparency of their wings make them a favorite subject matter of jewelry makers, artists and photographers.

Dragonflies and damselflies look primitive and ancient because they are; they've been around for a long time. In flight they look like a cross between a sleek fighter jet and a helicopter. Dragonflies and damselflies lay their eggs in or near water. Hatched larvae go through a series of molts as they grow. The eggs hatch after three to five weeks into nymphs called naiads, which are the aquatic larva or nymph of a dragonfly. The naiads live buried in the mud or attached to submerged plants for up to one to three years. The insect order Odonata includes not only the true dragonflies but also a closely related group known as damselflies.

We see larger populations of dragonflies when fresh water levels are high for a few years. As a novice entomologist and air traffic control enthusiast, I notice years when the air space is aflutter and can usually trace it back to weather patterns of the previous year or two. When things aren't "normal" we notice and want answers.

We always seem to be seeking for what is "normal" ... if there is such a thing. We do that because it gives us a sense of comfort. I track the water levels on the Great Lakes because I live on the lake shore and visually can see the rise and fall of Lake Michigan water levels through the seasons and the years. Record water levels in 2019/2020 gave rise to significant shoreline erosion. With 22,300 square miles of water, Lake Michigan is a natural freshwater wonder. The water levels continued to rise until May 2020 levels were at record heights. Water levels reached 51 inches above chart datum of 577.50 above sea level. On May 1st 2020 water level was 581.79 which was 2 inches above the record May level set in 1986. That's significant when you consider each inch of water on Lake Michigan is estimated to be 400 billion gallons of water! With record water levels comes erosion along the lake shore. Each erosion episode leaves intricate patterns in the sand as walls of sand erode and cave in.

I was thinking of this quote by photographer Jay Maisel while walking the Lake Michigan shoreline and observing the intricate detail of the erosion along the edge of the water. The remnants of patterns in the sand, after a storm wind erosion event, looked as though a team of archaeologists, complete with shovels, buckets and trowels, had carefully sifted a find in search of lost clues to an ancient city.

> *"As people, we love pattern. But the interrupted pattern is more interesting."*

In life, things can be rolling along, and we can become complacent and less understanding of the details, the wonder, and the beauty we have been gifted. When the pattern is interrupted we pay attention. We can use it as an opportunity to bring things into a better focus. While dealing with erosion and change we can renew our wonder with something as simple as a grain of sand.

The societal turmoil all around us in 2020 seemed to visually comport with the erosion caused by water levels and the helpless feeling that this is outside our control. It certainly was not normal. The dictionary definition for the phrase "shifting sands" is to describe something that changes frequently making it difficult to deal with or to make plans. Sounds like life in the year 2020. The Bible definition would sound something like this:

> *"... I made the sand a boundary for the sea,*
> *an everlasting barrier it cannot cross. The*
> *waves may roll, but they cannot prevail; they*
> *may roar, but they cannot cross it."*
> *– Jeremiah 5:22 (NIV)*

In a year of erosion and virus I take heart in that verse.

For navigational safety, depths on a chart are shown from a low-water surface or a low-water datum called chart datum. Chart datum is selected so that the water level will seldom fall below it, and only rarely will there be less depth available than what is portrayed on the chart. In non-tidal waters, chart datum is set so that the water level will be above datum approximately 95% of the time.

The water level of a lake or river is always changing due to variations in supply and discharge or in meteorological conditions. Dry and wet periods in many drainage basins, such as the Great Lakes, seem to occur in several-year cycles, causing

I Need to Change My Plants

corresponding periods of low and high water. Chart datum must be set with the low-stage years in mind and may appear pessimistically low during high-stage years.

On most lakes a single, level surface is adopted as chart datum over the entire lake. Along a river, chart datum is a sloping surface that approximates the slope of the river surface at low stage.

In non-tidal waters, chart datums are often assigned an elevation on some vertical reference system. In non-tidal waters such as the Great Lakes, heights of islands, clearances and elevation of lights are given above chart datum. Therefore, a knowledge of the present water level relative to chart datum is required to correct these chartered heights and all depths to the current conditions.

Rising water levels unearthed a shipwreck off shore near my home in the turtle position belly up.

I put on my waders and work my way into the cold November waters. My imagination pictures a 2-masted schooner from the 1880s about 90 feet in length and 20 feet wide ... a proud and stout wooden vessel of beams and iron, a flat-bottomed hull, an ideal sailing vessel for visiting shallow harbors. With a draft of only 5 to 7 feet, at 120 gross tons and economical to operate, shuttling lumber to Chicago from West Michigan she was subject to the November gales without the benefit of weather forecasting like we have today.

But alas no such drama. The wreck was a scow (barge) being towed that sank south of Muskegon while transporting a steam crane in November of 1936. We now know the archaeological piece of maritime history "shipwreck" exposed by erosion near my home is that of a flat-bottomed barge, which some believe possibly sank in 1936 and may have been built in the late 1800s. Time and erosion have uncovered the mishap and ... the rest is history.

It is

So, truly, what is chart datum normal? Datum is also the Latin word for given, thus, "It is." What is and what was is this: being lonely for a sustained period of time can be bad for one's physical and mental wellbeing. Isolation can make humans irritable, depressed and self-centered. And loneliness and the associated stress hormones like cortisol can contribute to sleeplessness, weight gain and anxiety. Locked down and lonely surrounded by a world of uncertainty can have serious effects on our mental and physical health.

Maintaining a garden engages the body, mind, and senses. All three together are a win-win-win for mental and physical health. All three create a position of mindfulness. In the moment.

Plants came to the rescue again in 2020. They are there to nurture. Our need to nurture is evident by the number of nice people who overwater their plants. Over the past few years many have rediscovered the need to be surrounded by plants and the need to nurture, the need to care and the companionship they offer.

Plants provide a remedy for many ailments both physical and mental. Doctors should be writing prescriptions for gardening.

Gardening is therapy because it makes you feel better. And when you feel better it spreads to others. It's contagious.

We need to have our hands in the dirt. Mycobacterium vaccae is a non-pathogenic bacterium that lives in soil. Research has shown this bacterium to have antidepressant benefits. Organisms that serve to regulate our immune system and suppress inappropriate inflammation. The concept is to study our loss of contact with non-pathogenic organisms in soil and the effect of their existence. As humans move away from farms or agricultural settings or hunter-gatherer existence into concrete and digital cities, does it put us at higher risk for inflammatory disease and stress-related issues? Mycobacterium vaccae, the bacteria found in soil, is theorized to enhance stress busting serotonin-releasing neurons in the brain when inhaled.

We instinctively and naturally realize, wherever you live on this planet, that plants, soil, cultivation and nurture in our lives is more than essential. It is quintessential.

20 reasons plants, gardens, landscapes are even more than essential ... they are quintessential.

1. First, foremost and most obvious ... plants are food. And we should have more of them in our diet. Eat more plants. We can boost the immune system with healthy vegetables, fruits and herb plants.

2. Plants improve air quality. And as we've learned we all want to breathe a little easier. And that's both outdoors and indoors, as indoor plants or "jungalows" improve our air at home and work too.

3. Gardens and landscapes reduce community crime and provide a common space for community cohesion. Residents feel greater pride in the beauty of where they live and rally together to maintain it. Plants bring people together.

4. Time outdoors in the landscape improves human performance and energy. Spending time in nature gives people an increased feeling of vitality, increasing their energy levels and making them feel more

animated.

5. Reduce stress. Participation in gardening and landscaping activities is an effective way to reduce levels of stress.

6. The garden, landscape and natural environments can improve mental health. People who spend more time outside in nature have a significantly more positive outlook on life than people who spend a great deal of time indoors.

7. Therapeutic effects of gardening. Gardening can have therapeutic effects on people who have undergone either mental or physical trauma. I would go so far as to say that flowers improve relationships and build compassion. Plants and flowers affect the level of compassion that people feel towards others. Studies have shown that people who spend more time around plants are much more likely to try and help others, and often have more advanced social relationships.

8. Plant roots reduce soil erosion. And bare soil is not a natural condition, something is going to grow there so be proactive. It may as well be beneficial.

9. We can reduce stormwater runoff and improve water quality with plant material. Green spaces absorb water in two ways: above the surface through the leaves and below ground through the root system.

10. How about your wallet? Energy savings anyone? Planting trees and other ornamental plants around a building can significantly reduce the sun's radiation effect on the temperature of the outer walls and lower

the associated cost of energy for heating and cooling. Plants provide insulating windbreaks in winter.

11. Health and recreation. Plants reduce health-care costs. Residents of an area with urban green spaces benefit from improved physical fitness and exercise outdoors.

12. Most cities are largely composed of cement and asphalt, which absorb heat from the sun's rays during the daylight hours. These "heat islands" can be offset with a balance of plant material.

13. Plants reduce noise pollution.

14. Flowers generate happiness.

15. Concentration and memory. The calming influence of natural environments is conducive to positive work environments by increasing a person's ability to concentrate on the task at hand.

16. Plants are like many other topics ... we never stop learning, and that's a good activity to promote.

17. Plants can accelerate the healing process. Trees, plants and flowers have a practical application in hospitals: the presence of plants in patient recovery rooms or outside the window have been shown to reduce the time necessary to heal.

18. Plant material attracts wildlife. As an example, consider the protective cover plant material provides wild birds visiting our yards.

19. We are always looking for ways to celebrate and to acknowledge others. Plants and flowers make the perfect gift or atmosphere for celebration.

20. Plants provide materials to harvest to build and for construction. Shelter. Agriculture, trees and plants always have and always will be an important part of our local community, state and national economic health and commerce creating jobs for many people across our nation.

The seed aeronautic
To kids is hypnotic
They fly and flutter
End up in a gutter
Their dispersal can be quite chaotic

Chapter Eight
Tactical Dispersal

IN SPENDING TIME WITH MY MILITARY friends I am amused by their use of acronyms. Acronyms are a way of military life that could duly compete with the acronyms, emojis and abbreviations of a texting teenager. And of course when faced with the societal conundrum of social distancing during a crisis, the Army coins a phrase all their own **"Tactical Dispersal."** As the Army got back to its business of combat training during the pandemic crisis, it had to be with social distancing, or what the Army calls tactical dispersal. As an example, sleeping cots would be placed 6 feet apart and soldiers would alternate how they sleep, no longer head to head. If anyone can figure out tactical dispersal techniques I'm sure the Army can because there is a right way, a wrong way and the Army way.

When it comes to nature, many plants also employ tactical dispersal techniques. Copious amounts of seed are produced by some plants increasing the odds that some will find success germinating in a new location. Seed is dispersed by wind, consumption by animals and the eventual evacuation through their digestive system or dispersal via moving water like streams. Plants like the dandelion or trees like the cottonwood have seeds that are light and have feathery bristles or loosely held together fibers like "cotton" or "snow" to be carried long distances by the wind. The numerous cottony fibers that accumulate create a June snowstorm on a breezy day. Since only a tiny fraction of seedlings survive, cottonwoods produce very large numbers of seeds. A seed in the center falls out soon after the cotton-like transport hits the ground, if not already shed before the dispersed delivery vehicle has fallen. While this method of tactical dispersion and shotgun approach works well from the tree's point of view, it can make them unpopular with people. It is sure to clog your air conditioning unit, cover your screens and end up in your car when the windows are rolled down. In the case of Cottonwood the snow lasts for only a couple weeks during which while jogging I need to remind myself to keep my mouth shut.

The most interesting form of tactical dispersion in my mind is the aeronautic movement and avigation of maple tree seed. As kids we called them "helicopters" or "whirligigs," but technically they are samaras or winged seeds produced by maple trees. The wing delivers the seed which germinates inside of its casing and then breaks free of it as the plant grows. A samara is a dry indehiscent fruit with a casing or wall that extends to one side in a wing-like shape – in some plants the wing extends to both sides of the seed. Some samara fruits split into two wings, technically two samaras, while others simply form one samara per fruit. The wing causes the fruit or seed to move through the air while spinning, like a helicopter. Maples are not the only tree employing this technique, using the wind to travel farther. In the case of maple trees they have a large dense shade canopy, so the seed is more successful finding a new home away from the parent as opposed to simply falling to the ground like a nut.

Annual crops of helicopters are cyclical and alternate bearing "inventories" contingent on weather conditions and stress on the tree in the past year. Obviously, trees do their reproductive thing on a regular basis, or they wouldn't still be here. This cyclical feat is referred to as "masting" or "mast seeding" where they bear a heavy seed crop. Maple trees that are healthy sometimes skip a year in seed formation, either due to poor pollination or to an exceptionally good growing season the year before. A plethora of samaras sometimes means the tree experienced some sort of "stress" the previous year, so producing a bumper crop of seeds is the tree's way of carrying on the species, should that stress continue and that particular tree not survive.

In bumper crop years the swirling seeds rain down on garden beds, mulched landscapes, lawns, decks, roofs, gutters and car vents. Along the lines of the natural evolution of man-made technology, I miss the pivoting vent windows in cars that disappeared sometime in the 1980s. The windows were known as poor-man's air conditioning and their triangular shape were great for inadvertently catching your sleeve and tearing it. They were great for catching airborne seeds in route and collecting them on the floor mat, dashboard and seats. Gutters are great seed collection devices. Who hasn't marveled at the bumper crop of helicopters spewed out at the base of a downspout after a gutter-flushing rainstorm.

The maple samaras are a natural lesson in aerodynamics. With a long wing that balances the weight of the seed, maple seeds are perfectly designed for flight. Since the seeds don't fall away from the tree until they're dry, they're very light, which helps them travel farther. If you examine a maple seed closely, you'll notice that the wing gets wider further away from the seed. When the seed spins, the air moving over the wide end of the wing moves faster than the air closer to the seed, which gives the seed the lift it needs to stay aloft. Then there are the veins on the leading edge of the wing, which generate just enough turbulence to help it cut through the air. The end result is a tiny tornado lowering the gravitational pressure above the samara and giving it lift to travel far and wide.

Once the maple seed has come in for a landing the work of the wings is not done. The "helicopter" wing helps it slide and stand upright between blades of grass or other vegetation it is competing with. Upright seeds are exposed to more light and have a better chance of embedding themselves into the soil below. As they settle into their new location, the spent wings are no longer useful like spent rocket stages on a moon launch and the seed germinates. For homeowners reluctantly growing this new crop of maples in their lawn, they can just mow the grass normally. After a few mowings and resultant removal of the foliage tops of these seedlings, they will eventually give up.

Invasive dispersals create a "new normal."

John Bartram of Philadelphia first introduced Norway maples from England to the U.S. in 1756. In doing so, the tree, with its copious seed production, joined native tree species as a component of eastern forest ecosystems. Norway maple forms monotypic or monoculture stands by displacing native trees, shrubs, and herbaceous understory plants. Not necessarily allopathic like a walnut tree, it's the canopy of dense shade that prevents regeneration of native seedlings. Native maples like sugar maple, *Acer saccharum* and red maple, *Acer rubrum*, or the developed varieties of these trees would be good substitutes for the Norway maple. The "invasion" of this tree however changed eastern forest inventories creating a new normal.

The presence of Norway Maple some would argue is a more subtle or palatable non-native arrival than other species. Take as an example the callery pear, first brought to the United States from China in 1908; it was highly resistant to fire blight and used as a rootstock onto which varieties of desirable pear trees could be grafted. The tree eventually made its way as the cultivar "Bradford" from the 1960s to now lining cookie-cutter suburbs and their penchant for uniformity.

If you follow the crowd you won't get much further than the crowd.

Since that time, the weak-limbed tree prone to storm damage is ubiquitous in city landscapes, evident by the copious canopies of white blooms lining streets everywhere in spring. What's wrong with the beautiful autumn leaf color and white spring blooms you ask? Ask anyone who has caught a whiff of trees in their full glory to tell you why. As polarizing as the scent of paperwhite narcissus or cilantro, the aroma has been likened to the scent of rotting fish with a hint of ammonia. The least of our troubles many would say as we have bigger fish to fry.

Invasive species of plants, animals and insects can change the landscape and "normalcy" in short order.

The macabre optics of swarms of dark birds wreaking havoc is enough to cause nightmares or a Hollywood movie plot. Hundreds of writhing Asian carp fish jumping out of the water and into the boat belting you in the head and causing concussions. Or vines that grow so fast you have to keep your window rolled up at a stop sign on a country road. Kudzu, Garlic Mustard, Dames Rocket, Purple Loosestrife, a deliberately imported seed and released through contaminated cargo ship ballast. Emerald Ash Borer decimated neighborhoods once lined with ash trees. Gypsy Moths. Asian Longhorned Beetles, Japanese beetles, Giant Hogweed, English Ivy, Japanese Knotweed and Sea Lampreys. The list goes on and on and on. Each a natural time bomb that explodes.

In the midst of the 2020 pandemic, unsolicited nondescript packages of seeds started showing up in the mailboxes of homes across the United States. Only makes sense in the year of "sow what's next?" My seeds were in a black and white package sent from Suzhou JiangSu China. The seeds inside looked like tiny mustard seeds. Not everyone received the same seed. The news spread faster than a bindweed vine with some theorizing it was an act of agricultural bio-terrorism. A "seedy" operation. I told people on my radio show not to plant them and not to dump them or flush them so they had an opportunity to sprout elsewhere. By planting any seeds from unknown origins doing so could introduce invasive species. Our state agricultural department was working on it when I called them, and it quickly became a federal and international investigation. The USDA, Homeland Security and APHIS, Animal and Plant health inspection service, all became involved due to the gravity, seriousness and consequence of invasive species to the agricultural and livestock industries. I immediately noticed on the packages sent there was no date stamp for when they were packed, sell by date and no lot number. A seed lot can be defined as a quantity of seed with every portion or every bag uniform within permitted tolerances. The seed lot or group is defined as the percentage of pure seed, inert matter, other crop seed, germination and dormant seed, weed seed, and rate of occurrence of noxious weed seeds.

These invasion issues create "a new normal" for all the *pandēmos* (from pan 'all' + dēmos 'people') or all the people whether they realize it or not. The law of unintended consequences. The costs of damage and control are staggering and long term. And it takes a community collectively to deal with the problem. For evidence of the import and impact of invasives just ask Eugene and his little 2- to 3-ounce dark birds.

A "Featheral" Offense

It was a beautiful autumn evening on October 4, 1960. Eastern Airlines Flight 375 lined up to take off from runway 9 at Boston Logan Airport. The Eastern Air lines turboprop Lockheed L-188 Electra, with four prop engines, was working its way down the east coast, having arrived from New York City, picking up passengers in Boston on its way to a final destination of Atlanta. It would never get there. The pilot, Captain C. W. Fitts, points the plane towards Winthrop Bay and throttles up the engines. The plane including crew had 72 passengers aboard when it began its flight and it would last less than 30 seconds after leaving the ground. The plane, once in the air and heading toward Winthrop, wouldn't get more than 200 feet off the ground before it plunged into the bay, tragically killing all but 10 on board. Investigations determined the plane struck a flock of birds just as it left the ground. European starlings were strewn across the runway and the surrounding area. It was later estimated that three of the plane's four engines had ingested a number of birds, causing the catastrophic failure and tragic result. Since that event the FAA and National Transportation Safety Board have worked on control of birds and wildlife surrounding airports in earnest with many means of strategy to avoid airplane and wildlife interference.

Migratory birds in flight, not "airport wildlife," more specifically migratory Canada geese, caused US Airways Flight 1549 to ditch in New York's Hudson River on January 15, 2009. The incident, since made into a Hollywood movie, was about an Airbus A320 and its now famous Captain Sully which, in the climbout after takeoff from New York City's LaGuardia Airport, struck a flock of Canada geese less than five miles northwest of the airport, and consequently lost all engine power. Canada geese are big and when sucked into an engine can be destructive. I've seen some refer to them as flying cows with an unrelenting quest for food. Anyone with a lawn near a body of water like a pond can attest to the volume and size of the droppings these birds create. The migratory birds are among the largest species of bird in North America, with an estimated weight of about 8 pounds each. It only takes a few to make an impact on an airplane engine comparatively to the "flock" of 2- to 3-ounce starlings that tragically brought down Eastern Airlines Flight 375 in 1960.

I Need to Change My Plants

> *"What's done cannot be undone."*
> *– William Shakespeare in Macbeth*

That brings us to Eugene Schieffelin, a 19th-century drug manufacturer and Shakespeare fanatic. On a chilly morning on March 6, 1890, Schieffelin released cages containing a total of 60 loud, black birds never before seen in North America at New York City's Central Park. Rumor has it he later released another 40 starlings imported from Europe. The cost at the time was not "cheep" and the economic impact years later was enormous. At the time, non-native imports and their impact was not understood. From the few birds in the 1890s to the hundreds of millions in North America today, the agricultural damage is immense. Their destruction is particularly perspicacious because they congregate in massive flocks, known as murmurations, which can number in the hundreds of thousands. It was such a murmuration theorized to bring down Eastern Airlines flight 375.

Why did he do it? Eugene had set out to introduce every bird mentioned in Shakespeare's plays to America. He was part of the American Acclimatization Society, a New York City group founded with the purpose of importing European plants and animals to the United States. In the case of European starlings the end result was millions of dollars in crop damage every year and the spread of disease. And to think Shakespeare had only briefly mentioned the bird in *Henry IV.* "Nay, I'll have a starling shall be taught to speak; Nothing but Mortimer, and give it to him." That's it, that's all. The starling's brief moment of fame.

The end result of Eugene's esteem for William Shakespeare and his bird transplants was years of agricultural financial damage. The Starling imports were able to survive and thrive as weaker birds were not, because they're not captious crows and finicky eaters and willing to feed on a wide array of insects and plants. They are not picky on where they live and are willing to roost almost anywhere. This allows them to conveniently coexist with humans in both urban and rural settings from high rises to farms. The rest is history as you can find these marauders across the entire United States and beyond. Starlings, after all, are incredible mimics, adept at copying almost everything and quite obnoxiously to boot.

Newton was right. For every action, there is an equal and opposite reaction ... when the agendas are different. In the third law, when two objects interact, they apply forces to each other of equal magnitude and opposite direction. A tug of war. Not a war in that sense of the word or a coup d' etat, but a struggle, a vexation for all when unintended consequences result.

It is a reminder that today the world is a smaller place, and actions and reactions can have a wide-reaching effect. So choose carefully. We inhabit this earth together. Together we have to make it work. Whether plants or people, a virus seems to know when we are divided and attacks weak points. It's a good reminder to consider your actions, protect and care for the weak and to love your neighbor as yourself.

Living in symbiosis
With mutual positive focus
Let's be symbionts
In positive response
And benefit from our closeness

Chapter Nine

Get Busy Lizzy

WE WANT COLOR. MOST OF US have a favorite color and it's a means to distinguish ourselves from others. It's "your" color as an individual, never mind the fact that a color belongs to no one. My favorite is blue which doesn't gain me individualistic points due to the fact it is the world's favorite color. If you want to take the personality out of it and pick something less risky to avoid complaints, you could choose grey or beige. The combination of grey and beige creates a color called greige. This humdrum backdrop became popular with the advent of flipping houses and building equity. That's the beauty of flowering annual plants or "bedding" plants. They are with us for a season and give license to be daring with something much better than monotonous. You can exhibit polychromatic personality without peril to your pocketbook and find purpose in the activity to boot. Activity with plants and colors keep us young and engaged. Allan Armitage, a friend and famous horticulturist, stated it this way. "Gardening simply does not allow one to be mentally old, because too many hopes and dreams are yet to be realized."

What you focus on ... will be.

Some plants are notorious for not blooming if pampered too much. Trumpet Vine, wisteria, morning glories, or impatiens as examples, if pampered don't bloom as well as they could and don't bother in lieu of continuous foliage growth. You have to change their focus. In nature, plants bloom to produce seeds that guarantee the survival of the species, thus ensuring the next generation. When under stress or under a significant change a plant focuses on reproduction and it blooms.

What you focus on ... will be. If you focus on fear you will be afraid. If you focus on failure you won't see opportunity. It doesn't always knock. Focus is important, especially in a crisis. That's why some people thrive in a crisis as they focus on it as inevitable change.

Over time I have learned that sometimes "losses" or failures can be sweeter than the victories. Why? because I benefited the most from them.

When I was young working at a garden center as a teenager I always liked impatiens, which would compete for attention with the sacrosanct presence of geraniums and the ubiquitous omnipresent petunia. This made me happy, because deadheading geraniums and petunias before today's "self cleaning" hybridized sterile varieties was not a fun job. Sticky, sweet, slimy spent petunia blossoms and the never-ending "dead heading" or pinching of geraniums seemed endless. My tutelage in flowering annuals was directed by a no-nonsense hard-driving spirited enterprising lady who had no time for excuses.

I was trained and supervised as a youngster at the garden center by an owner named Doris who was a Navy WAVE from 1943 to 1946 during WWII. The acronym WAVES meant Women

Accepted for Voluntary Emergency Service, and those who volunteered had to serve for the duration of the war plus six months. On July 30, 1942, President Franklin Delano Roosevelt signed Public Law 689 creating the women's reserve as a part of the Navy and war effort. As a 19-year-old kid deadheading flowering annuals and setting displays at the store there was no question who was the captain of the ship in my work area.

To avoid scuttlebutt everything was to be ship-shape. Each day it was ahoy and all hands on deck for inspection: something like a floral boot camp. You could hear her coming, working in the plant area in a dress and heels with a floppy sun hat and gloves. Click, click, click you would hear the rapid footsteps of her heels on the concrete floor as she approached and everyone stood at attention. I was trying to stay out of the brig even though it was only a rumor that one existed. After inspections she would type a report on site using an old typewriter in the office. Rat tat tat tat it sounded like a machine gun as the keys would strike the paper. She would rip the paper off the typewriter and distribute her orders for the day. She would then jump in to the work with the rest of us pitching and slinging plants into position and identifying those that needed to go to "sick bay" for recovery or discounting. At the time she was in her early 60s and it was tough to keep up with her pace. At the end of the day she would go back to the typewriter to hammer out a synopsis of the work yet to be done and where improvement was needed. The notes were random and urgent with a mix of capital letters and odd spacing, giving them the feel of a hybrid between a Western Union telegraph and a ransom note.

Frequently on the worklist, she would instruct me to clean my work closet, referring to it as Fibber McGee's closet. Fibber McGee and Molly was a very popular 1935-1959 American radio comedy series. A running gag on the show was the hall closet. It involved McGee opening a cacophonous closet and the ensuing avalanche of hodgepodge and jumble crashing down on him and

Molly. "I gotta get that closet cleaned out one of these days" was his usual response, and, of course, just as with my closet "one of these days" never arrived, taking a backseat to more pressing issues at hand.

As time went on I got older, Doris retired and plant material got better. I was so happy to see plant breeders develop petunias in the "no-need-to-deadhead" category. Prior to improvements by plant developers, pinching out all those faded flowers on a petunia, with its stems that are so disagreeably sticky, has never been a lot of fun. Petunias that bloom nonstop without deadheading are replacing the old petunias that needed deadheading and mid-season rejuvenation. That's because many of today's nonstop flowering annuals are sterile varieties. When plants are bred sterile and unable to produce seed they are "self cleaning" with the flowers falling off as they age.

By deadheading a plant repeatedly like flowering annuals, it's often possible to force it to bloom again and again. However if the plant is bred for sterile blooms, the flowers it produces don't result in viable seeds. The plant will bloom again and again, striving futilely to produce seed and putting on an impressive season-long show for you. Thanks to hybridization and selection, the selection and quality of annual flowers just keeps on improving, year after year. Unlike my teen and young adult years at the garden center, where hours were spent pinching, we are now at the point where deadheading is often no longer necessary.

Impatient for progress

At the time and for decades *Impatiens walleriana* was arguably the most popular spring and summer flowering annual on earth. The genus name Impatien comes from a Latin word meaning impatient as in the violent seed discharge from the ripe seed pods. It surpassed the ever present Geranium, Petunia or Marigold in popularity, because it would bloom in the shade, was floriferous and came in a number of different bright colors. Large monoculture swaths would be planted creating a blaze of color for the summer months. Appropriate enough, Doris would refer to them as "Busy Lizzy's" as we would stock the tables with flowers at a pace that would make one dizzy. As a baby "bloomer" a lot of my work experiences and ensuing ethic would be influenced by those who had experienced both the Great Depression and World War II.

One influence I never personally met was the "Father of Impatiens" whose name was Claude Hope. Not Bob Hope, Claude Hope, but thanks for the memories nonetheless. In 1941, when the Japanese bombed Pearl Harbor, Mr. Hope was working for the federal Agriculture Department in Maryland. He was drafted into the Army and immediately put to work on a project to develop an American supply of quinine, needed to treat malaria among soldiers fighting in the Pacific. Claude was sent to Costa Rica with the sprouted seeds for *Cinchona ledgeriana*, from which quinine was made, and asked to help create a cinchona farm. After the war he decided to stay in Costa Rica and start a seed company.

In the 1960s, after years of development, he turned the wild rangy impatien plant into a more compact, marketed and reliable bedding plant soon to be planted under trees, in window boxes and hanging baskets throughout America. Many feel it was his influence and the ubiquitous impatiens that changed the face of American gardening. He developed a plant more suitable to the homeowners' need for color around the home. I remember the Elfin series of impatiens followed later by the "Super Elfins." Other introductions named Accent, Tempo, Cajun series soon followed. And why not, the impatiens, with their colorful flowers and shade tolerance, became the most popular flowering annual among consumers. Growers liked them too with good germination, uniform habit and fast-finishing speed making them a profitable crop to turn. And "turn" they did, as everywhere you looked the omnipresent drifts of impatiens were planted from the suburbs to the cities to commercial sites as well. They were everywhere in colorful abundance. After decades of colorful success we took a "Laissez Faire" approach that they would always be there. But when monocultures are encouraged and diversity is not practiced like the rows of Ash trees that lined our neighborhoods and were wiped out by emerald ash borer, lessons are always to be learned. Sometimes the hard way.

Disease changes everything

Things changed in a matter of months for the home landscape in 2012 due to a plant disease. With many problems like a disease we don't see it coming. When it arrives and the host (impatiens in this case) are widely planted, the problem spreads like wildfire and everything changes. That's what happened with "IDM" or impatiens downy mildew. Impatiens downy mildew or *Plasmopara obducens* is a disease caused by a fungus-like organism and had been known to be around for some time. Prior to that point it had been dormant and not much of a problem. How could a plant like impatiens, the colorful darling of the shade garden since the early 60s, suddenly be wiped out by disease? And how could it rapidly spread well beyond a region to numerous countries at the same time? Some say it was exceptionally cool, wet weather in Europe and Hurricane Irene in the eastern U.S. that created the perfect storm. Others say the plant's susceptibility combined with its "overplanted" monocultures did it in. In other words "over use" led to lack of plant "social distancing" and a monoculture host, the rest is history.

IDM spread like wildfire seemingly overnight stripping plants of both foliage and flower until yellow stalks were all that remained. Downy mildew can be spread short distances by water splashing from infected plants and greater distances by wind-borne spores from infected plants. The maddening infection is caused by both short-lived spores produced and seen in white downy-like growth on the undersides of infected leaves. The spores spread via wind with the ability to affect and then rapidly wipe out a stand of impatiens almost overnight when conditions are right. There are also spores, called oospores, that release into the soil from infected plant debris where they survive and affect future plantings of impatiens in the same bed. Can you say crop rotation is a good idea? Downy mildew can occur in beds with no history of the disease if wind-dispersed spores blow in from other locations. Once plants are infected they will not recover and are toast. We learned the disease went beyond pernicious and was incurable.

Pathologists and the plant industry were at a loss and sales slumped as news of the disease made headlines. The search was on for shade alternatives and people would have to familiarize themselves with plants like the begonia. As I would always say to the novice gardener, "No, begonia is not a foreign country." I love both fibrous and tuberous begonias, but they didn't have the color mix and inexpensive punch that flats of impatiens could afford. The search was on with a need for resistance to the disease and that can come from only two sources: a plant within the species that naturally exhibits resistance, or to cause a desired genetic mutation to occur.

Since 2012 it was time to get "busy Lizzy" as plant breeders were asked, "Can you breed IDM-resistant impatiens?" As is the case with most diseases, solutions first of all are not that easy, and secondly would take time to develop. But necessity is the mother of invention, and now years removed from the shock of leafless flowerless stalks worldwide hybridizers have made progress on new resistant varieties to position colorful impatiens for a comeback in suburbia USA. Remember crisis breeds opportunity. You just need time to recover, reset and reprioritize. Change can be rapid and inevitable, recovery just takes time.

If you need a prescription
But can't locate a physician
A dose of menthol
Can't prevent all
But may avoid a conniption

Chapter Ten

It's Good for What "Ales" You

When I was a kid, if I didn't feel well, Mom always had four solutions to *any* problem. Mom kept these options in her medicinal toolbox and readily prescribed:

> Vicks VapoRub
> Ginger Ale
> Baking Soda
> Saltine Crackers

The use of these remedies have stuck with me through the years becoming almost habitual in my adult years. It is said if a child breathes in an aroma for more than a few seconds, like the smell of lilacs in May, it is imprinted on your memory for life. Today, on occasion, I will put a little menthol vapor rub under my nose before bed because it is a stress reliever. Today, if I am found sipping on a ginger ale I'm asked, "do you feel sick?" I love ginger ale and tend to have a glass everyday. And today chicken soup isn't chicken soup unless it has saltine crackers floating in it. I like brushing my teeth with baking soda, it makes me feel wholesome.

Vaping is nothing new

The way that Vicks VapoRub "works" is by inhaling the vapors created by the rub, your brain is tricked into thinking you are breathing more easily. Does it actually relieve congestion or a cough? Or is your brain tricked into thinking it does because of the aroma produced? There is no direct evidence that putting Vicks VapoRub on your feet with warm socks will have any benefit either. Yet many people swear by this treatment and are sure that it cures their cold symptoms.

Vaping is nothing new. Mom used Vicks VapoRub to fix everything. She might not have an MD, PhD or DO after her name but she had to *DO* something. Often she would reach for the VapoRub from the medicine cabinet. At least she was doing something. These memories as kids have now caused us as adults to take it a little too far. I've seen it used as insect control, for mosquito bites, rubbed on the stomach for belly fat, coughs, chapped lips, warts, dandruff, toenail fungus and even for crying your way out of a speeding ticket. It's a world-wide phenomenon. In Asia it's called "Tiger Balm" a topical over-the-counter pain reliever that contains ingredients such as camphor, menthol, cajuput oil, and clove oil. It comes as a cream, gel, or liquid that is applied superficially to the area of pain and absorbed through the skin.

One plant that smells like Vicks VapoRub to me in summer is *Vitex agnus-castus*, commonly called "chaste tree lilac." It is grown in warm winter climates as a vase-shaped shrub, and in cold winter climates as a 3-5' tall herbaceous perennial. On a hot humid day the greyish-green leaves are aromatic and smell like my childhood memory of VapoRub. The fragrant, lavender to pale violet flowers are very attractive to butterflies. Another common name for the plant is monk's pepper. In medieval times the peppercorn-like fruit of the tree was used to blunt their libido and maintain their vows of chastity. Any tree that is called "chaste" like a monk is probably a trustworthy friend to have around and won't cause a lot of trouble. It also explains why you certainly aren't going to attract many suitors smelling like VapoRub.

Another plant that brings back the childhood memories of Mom prescribing VapoRub is the "Vicks Plant" *Plectranthus tomentosa*, a plant with leaves that smell like Vicks VapoRub or mentholatum when crushed. The leaves can be steeped in boiling water to vaporize the characteristic oils which are then inhaled, helping to clear nasal and respiratory passages.

The primary ingredients I see in the container of VapoRub on my bathroom counter are camphor (a cough suppressant and topical analgesic), eucalyptus oil (a cough suppressant) and menthol (a cough suppressant and topical analgesic). Thymol is an inactive ingredient.

Originally Vicks VapoRub was called Richardson's Croup and Pneumonia Cure Salve. Experimenting with menthols from Japan, Lunsford Richardson developed a strong-smelling ointment combining menthol, camphor, oil of eucalyptus, and several other oils, blended in a base of petroleum jelly. Lunsford Richardson realized that wasn't necessarily a user friendly name and to say the least fit the wording on a jar. Richardson changed the name to honor his brother-in-law, Dr. Joshua Vick. Others say he plucked the name from a seed catalog he'd been perusing that listed the Vick Seed Co. Smart move by an entrepreneur who may have gained some marketing savvy after previously inventing Vick's Tar Heel Sarsaparilla and Vick's Yellow Pine Tar Cough Syrup.

It wasn't necessarily the name change or marketing prowess that caused the rub to jump off the shelves. When the Spanish flu hit the U.S. in 1918, Vicks VapoRub was viewed as a medication to mitigate the effects, causing sales to more than triple in just one year. Sales increased so dramatically that the Vicks manufacturing plant operated day and night to keep up with orders.

The scientific knowledge of disease was far enough along in 1918 that people knew to clean surfaces and that the disease could be spread through a sneeze, a cough or droplets in the air. But in the confusion of a pandemic there were unfounded theories that using Vicks Vaporub, drinking alcohol or gargling salt water were remedies. There were even those who thought the flu could be transmitted over the phone.

Let's botanically break down a few of the elements that make VapoRub, that bouquet of balm, the aura of aroma that odorous incense redolent of mint overload brain freeze.

Mentha or Mint is a well-known genus in the Lamiaceae family that has medicinal and aromatic value. The Mentha genus includes numerous species that are widely grown in temperate areas around the world. There is peppermint *Mentha x piperita* and spearmint *Mentha spicata* and so many fun flavors of mint from pineapple to citrus, chocolate to apple. It is the Japanese mint *Mentha arvensis,* popularly known as menthol mint, corn mint, field mint or wild mint that is a source of natural menthol widely used in pharmaceutical and flavour industries. Mint has been used through the years as a remedy for respiratory illnesses like bronchitis, sinusitis and the common cold as it acts as an excellent expectorant.

If you're thinking about planting mint for the first time, keep in mind that it spreads, given space and water. Mint can make anyone a green thumb. Its roots, properly called rhizomes, run underground and can send up shoots many feet away from the mother plant. You can label it and accept compliments on its robust growth. Without boundaries they might require a new zip code after a few years. The aroma is great but the plant is a little bit of a bully. You have to admire their tenacity. To control it you would be wise to take these steps:

- Contain mint by planting it in pots.
- Create deep soil barriers for mint to limit its spread. A bottomless bucket, barrel or container sunk into the ground will work
- Plant mint in less than ideal growing conditions to slow its growth.

So what have we learned so far?

1. I have to *assume* the Great Wall of China is visible from space because I've never been to space, and
2. mint is invasive.

Cinnamomum camphora, the camphor tree is native to regions in Asia. The camphor tree is one I've never tried to grow because it takes a lot of room. I've heard of tree canopies over 100 feet wide. A broad oval canopy can produce a lot of shade. It also won't grow in Michigan, needing a warmer climate such as zone 9 or warmer. The waxy substance that is used to make camphor oil from this tree is a key ingredient in ointments ideal to relieve muscle pains and joint pains while inhalation relieves bronchial congestion. The strong menthol fragrance comes from the bark of the camphor tree. If you need a nose tingling fragrance you're barking up the right tree.

Eucalyptus oil is the generic name for distilled oil from the leaf of Eucalyptus native to Australia. People use eucalyptus as a decongestant when they have a cold, ideal in cough drops or tea. Eucalyptus is a natural pest deterrent but to most humans it has a pleasant smell. I'm most familiar with it using it in dried or fresh floral bouquets. If you're an allergy sufferer this might be the bunch to bring home in a bouquet.

You have thyme on your hands.

One of the "inactive ingredients" in my beloved VapoRub is Thymol extracted from *Thymus vulgaris*. As a person rooted in botanical nomenclature, I immediately recognize something as "vulgaris" to be considered "common." *Thymus vulgaris* or thymol was used by physicians while combating the hookworm epidemic, which struck the workers building the St. Gotthard Tunnel in the Alps during 1879-1880. A difficult project, many deaths occurred in its construction for a number of reasons. It was one of the first large-scale projects using dynamite as a means to an end. Probably a poor choice of words. Let's just say the excavation of the tunnel was enhanced by the use of explosives expediting its construction. Aside from a variety of construction mishaps causing death, there were also serious health issues caused by an epidemic of hookworm infections. Thymol was isolated by scientists with *thyme* on their hands, and the rest was history with major advances in parasitology.

Green Thumb

I'm also a fan of effervescent tablets, and my friend Ignaz inspires me and thankfully many in history to have clean hands. Let me explain. Ignaz Semmelweis was a Hungarian physician who, through statistical analysis, determined that rigorous hand-washing rules for doctors and surgeons was an important medical practice, particularly in the maternity ward. "Scrubbing up" by surgeons is a well-established practice, but it wasn't always that way in the 1800s. It took Ignaz to figure out that disease and death were significantly reduced by the simple act of hand washing. Thank you Ignaz for all the lives you have saved.

As gardeners we understand the phrase "Dirty hands clean money." Dirty hands are the sign of honesty, though not necessarily clean, work and labor and thus the income from such work is what we could call clean money. More than just our green thumb we need to clean our fingers. But the nails can be tough to clean. That's where Alka Seltzer or cold tablets that fizz in water come into play. Effervescent or carbon tablets are tablets which are designed to dissolve in water, and release carbon dioxide. They are products of the compression of component ingredients in the form of powders into a dense mass and put in a hermetically sealed package. Tear the package open and plop them in water. An effervescent nail cleaner for a gardener with an upset stomach.

Good for what "ales" you

If you live in Michigan, you might have had a Vernors to drink. But if you live anywhere else, you probably have no idea what Vernors is. Some call it ginger ale, but let me tell you it is so much better than just ginger ale. Originally from Detroit, it's a soda or "pop" that Michiganders can call their own ... a real taste treat. If you're queasy it is understood that the impulse to fight nausea is mitigated by a can of ginger ale or Vernors. It's more than psychological, but I'm not a human doctor so I can't prove it. I crack open a can often causing others to ask if I'm feeling sick. A professional caregiver would reach for a ginger ale as an antiemetic. In layman's terms that means a preventative from vomiting. It's a bedside staple. My mom would give me a glass when I wasn't feeling well. I drink it because I love the taste. The apple doesn't fall far from the tree because so does my 2 year old grandson Max. Instead of "Vernors" he calls it "Burners." He reaches for the can and says, "let's have a burners Papa" then burps and smiles.

People smarter than me and above my pay grade have determined the spice ginger is at least marginally effective against nausea caused by the flu, overeating or motion sickness. Ginger has been cultivated since days of old and was the remedy for a host of ailments including nausea. I'm sure ginger was part of 19th century traveling medicine shows. When the customer got heartburn the snake oil salesman and his miracle elixirs had already moved on to the next town. Ginger since ancient times has played a role in being good for what ails us.

Pharmacists played a role in the development of ginger ale. It was the Detroit pharmacist James Vernor in the mid 1800s who created the recipe of ginger, vanilla, and spices and left it in an oak barrel, resulting in the magical treat we enjoy even today. According to lore and legend, when Vernor left to serve in the Civil War, he had a stash of his experimental ginger ale syrup base in an oak cask. When he returned from the war he opened the keg and found the drink had changed through the aging process. He declared it "Deliciously different," which became the drink's motto. Some discredit the legend saying the development was well after the Civil War, but it makes a great story nonetheless.

It was in the early 1900s a Canadian pharmacist John J. McLaughlin, created a pale "dry" ginger ale you may have heard of called Canada Dry. A variation on a theme from north of the border, and a little less sweet than the Detroit creation.

Ginger ale was a popular soda especially during Prohibition, as it was an ideal mixer for illicit liquor. Ginger ale could make your booze go further with a kick. There are those who question if there is real ginger in these drinks or if it's just the psychological effects of carbonation. I'm sure there is real ginger in the sodas. They just aren't going to tell us how much. So I'll continue to take my ginger supplements. Still, people like me turn to ginger ale and ginger root when they are feeling under the weather. With the sky above aren't we always under the weather? That's why I have a ginger ale or Vernors almost everyday. Ginger certainly makes for a great female name, I'm sure popularized by the sultry actress in the *Gilligan's Island* episodes as Ginger Grant. Tina Louise was, I'm sure, the reason many tuned in on the show's run from 1964 to 1967. I was fascinated by the fact the professor,

Russell Johnson, as Professor Roy Hinkley could make a radio out of a coconut. It was one of those shows that got better as time went on into syndication. It aged well like James Vernor's oak barrels of deliciously different Vernors.

You "Cracker" me up

Talk about something simple. A dry cracker with salt on it. Cheap and easy, your Mom would give them to you to settle your stomach. Or, if the problem was a head cold, chicken soup was the solution with crackers floating on the top. The precursors were "soda crackers." Something known as pilot bread, they were similar to what sailors ate on their ships. It was dense and hard, but traditionally accepted as a cracker. They just added "saltine" I guess. Dense and hard with a touch of salt, if you were traveling it was light, easy and wouldn't spoil. So Mom would bring them on vacation too. In a pinch saltine crackers with peanut butter were dry and stuck to the roof of your mouth. Their filling expansion would stop the complaining about hunger for a while as Dad drove on to the vacation destination.

With a history that goes back to the 1800s and early 1900s it was the Great Depression that really catapulted their popularity. Americans didn't have much money and so the need for foods that were inexpensive but flavorful was evident. People could use these crackers as a filler in foods such as meatloaf to stretch out the amount, or use them with a soup to make the meal more filling, without spending a lot of money. Mom picked up on that, and the saltine cracker helped stretch the family budget and keep the kid's stomachs filled. To this day I eat saltine crackers when I feel depressed.

Fungus is soda pressing

As kids we would make sandbox volcanos using a water bottle mounded with sand and partially filled with water and bak-

I Need to Change My Plants

ing soda. When you added the missing ingredient, vinegar, you had an eruption. When the baking soda and the vinegar mix, they form a gas, producing a fizzing eruption forced out of the narrow opening of the bottle. By adding dish soap you could make it foam. The eruption was only contested by the reaction of Mom when she discovered the mess we had made raiding the kitchen pantry.

There are many formulations for plant fungicide using baking soda or sodium bicarbonate with vegetable oil and dish soap, bringing up the question: Which formulations are phytotoxic in and of themselves? If you damage the plant what good did your homemade fungicide do? I have even seen some go so far as to say the use of baking soda in the garden sweetens the taste of tomatoes. The first compound of baking soda, sodium, can burn roots, leaves and other plant parts. Like anything, maybe moderation, if you're convinced, would be the key. If you use it, try a test patch on your plants before spraying carte blanche. You may have to adjust concentration and dilution of your homemade solution so you don't burn any leaves. Typically the ratio is 3 tablespoons of baking soda to 1 gallon of water.

I myself am going to use copper and sulfur fungicides successful as a fungus control for plants through the ages. I'll stick with baking soda to brush my teeth, clean tile grout, put one in the refrigerator, dump some down the garbage disposal, and, like Mom, prescribe its use to remedy the occasional canker sore.

Want to feel better? Need a ginger ale? Some crackers? How about a little VapoRub? Will Baking soda fix it? Not interested in any of those solutions? Sorry Mom. Remember as I've said before, when all else fails plants provide a remedy for many ailments both physical and mental. I think doctors should be writing prescriptions for gardening. And you should change your plants.

Rick Vuyst

When facing a juggernaut
Here's some food for thought
Exercise and attitude
Will improve your mood
And is sure to improve your plot

Chapter Eleven
Improve Your Plot in Life

THE ADVENT OF THE INTERNET AND social media has made instant celebrities of some plants. Take the example of a plant like *Philodendron monster*a. There has been debate and speculation on why the plant naturally has holes in its foliage, like the holes in a slice of swiss cheese. Some have suggested that Monsteras native to tropical regions evolve and develop holes in their leaves to resist the strong winds of hurricanes. Plants like Strelitzia, better known as Bird of Paradise, split their leaves to allow wind through as well. Others have suggested the Philodendron, as it gains height, has the holes to better allow water to come in contact with their roots.

You might say the "hole theories" have holes in them. Wouldn't it be true then that all hurricane region tropicals would adapt and have holes in them? If the rainwater theory held water wouldn't more plants do that? And, if the plant is native to tropical rainforests where it rains a lot, would it really be necessary to be holey? There must be a better explanation for the "do what you need to do" adaptation with these plants ... a better explanation than healthy plants "shot" full of holes look interesting and make for a great social media post.

The slits or holes in the leaves is called fenestration. It may be the *Philodendron monstera* as an understory plant has adapted to maximize available light.

Monsteras vine up trees growing from the forest floor in an epiphytic way. Light can be at a premium with the plant trying to capture sunlight that makes it through the forest canopy.

A whole leaf and a fenestrated leaf can individually perform the same, but the "holey" leaf is able to share light with those below. The unique leaf structure and plant makes a sacrifice for the good of all, namely light for those below to survive. They understand that they and the understory plants are in this together.

It's the Hole truth

The whole truth is plants are amazing adapters and they do it all with little complaining. Plants such as Haworthias, a popular succulent plant for our homes, developed leaf fenestrations so leaf tips are transparent to allow light down into the plants when buried by the frequent sand and dust storms of their native South Africa. The humble plant Lithops also known as "living stones" improve their plot in life by adapting to their environment. They emulate stones in drought ridden regions of Africa to go undetected as a snack to foraging vegetation-consuming animals.

Change and adapt to what you have control to change and stop complaining about what you can't change. Improve your plot.

In the north we bond together by complaining about winter and the weather. It's hard to have a positive mindset in winter when we make small talk about how miserable and dark it is in winter. Or is it? Changing your mindset could make all the difference for both you and those surrounding your jolly old self. If we did what they do in northern Norway where it is cold and dark in winter, and celebrate it collectively instead, we "enjoy" instead of "endure" with an infectious positive approach. They have to adjust to an extreme environment when it comes to light. Even if fenestrated with windows, they have to endure something called Polar Night. During the Polar Night, which lasts from November to January, the sun doesn't rise at all. Tromsø, Norway, is home to extreme light variation between seasons. After Polar Night the days get progressively longer until the Midnight Sun period, from May to July, when it never sets. After the midnight sun, the days get shorter and shorter again until the Polar Night, and the yearly cycle repeats. **They go outside** instead of complaining about it indoors. Getting outside is a known mood booster. They have a mantra that there's no such thing as bad weather, only bad clothing. They embrace a word "koselig" that means a sense of coziness. It's cozy to know "we're all in this together" so let's make the most of it.

> *"People will forget what you said or did but people will never forget how you made them feel."*
>
> *– Maya Angelou*

I remember long meetings in a room where a piece of artwork on the wall set the tone for my personal disposition. The artwork depicted castles and bridges in Heidelberg Germany in the 15th century. In the southern area of Germany, between Frankfurt and Stuttgart, Heidelberg's location botanically allows for plants atypical of central and northern European climates. You might be lucky enough to find a fig, almond or olive tree there. I'm sure it's a very nice place. But the illustration hanging on the wall was dark with Medieval castles, moats, towers, people navigating row boats on the Neckar river and huddled to stay warm around smoldering fires. There was dark billowing smoke under the overpass of a stone arch bridge along the river, adding to the gloomy aphotic feel of the print. I know I need sunlight for my personal photosynthesis. Old arch bridges have been built since ancient times due to easy accessibility of stone masonry and an appropriate material for sustaining compressive forces. I found it depressive. The drab color of the framed artwork loomed large in this room. I would glance at the wall and in letters below the black and white 15th-century illustration it said "The wages of sin is death." I suppose the artwork accomplished its goal as I had a censurable guilty cloud over my head after spending time in that room. Culpable, I would seek forgiveness and move on.

Looking back it wasn't necessarily what was said, it was how it made me feel for the rest of the day.

Reinvest your "learnings"

A good standard to apply in life is to reinvest your profits. I have made a practice of that my entire life. When going through a crisis I guarantee you that you are going to learn. That is not a question. The

> **I need to change my plants:** When you change your attitude from "I didn't succeed" to "I'm growing" ... everything changes.

question is: What are you going to do with your "learnings?" You reinvest those "learnings" to both your benefit and the benefit of others. I remember my Dad working in the garden in October and November. The harvest was complete. He was reinvesting his earnings in the form of leaves off the trees tilling in the organic matter for future growth. On our suburban lawns in autumn, every leaf is sought out and blown, bagged, tagged, raked or disposed of. Why? Obviously nutrient concentration values vary considerably, but the big three, Nitrogen, Phosphorus and Potassium content are in the foliage. In addition essential micronutrients such as magnesium, calcium, iron, manganese, copper and zinc are present. The foliage in the woods contributes to long-term fertility as nutrients are released over time. The organic structure of the foliage requires microbial decomposition to release them. The benefit of organic matter improves the structure of the soil as well as increasing earthworm residence.

He needed to P

Hennig Brand was a German alchemist in the 17th century. Brand had an idea. Pursuit of that idea resulted in his contribution to both the periodic table and society. Legend has it he had an idea he could turn tinkle to gold. Yes urine to gold . He was so convinced he borrowed it from neighbors and went so far to put out bowls by taverns asking for contributions to his cause. This of course I'm sure was much to the chagrin of those who lived with him and his experimental antics. At the time, he thought you could change worthless materials into precious metals. He was going to distill gold from the golden substance we call pee.

Hennig used his second wife's money to build, not a lavatory, but a laboratory in the basement for processing his "fools gold." Legend has it with the help of his stepson he stockpiled as much as 1,500 gallons of urine. No word on what he paid his stepson to be his assistant or what that basement smell was like. I can only imagine. They would cook and boil, analyze, boil some more the collected beer drinkers tinkle in the gold-digging hopes he was right. Tinkle tinkle little star how I wonder what you are.

Curious minds throughout history have made surprise, unexpected miraculous discoveries all because they were, well ... curious. In the case of Hennig Brand and his search for gold the rest is history. He discovered and stumbled upon P as in the periodic table symbol for the chemical element phosphorus. He didn't make gold but rather a strange white, waxy substance that glowed in the dark. He discovered an element that would be used in the future for everything from deadly explosives to the synthetic fertilizers used to grow crops for hungry people worldwide.

Phosphate is a huge market. Most of it goes into fertilizer. You will find it as the compound calcium phosphate in baking soda. Phosphorus is used in everything from fine china to fireworks. Bright sparks and flashes in your 4th of July explosions are in part due to the element. A controversial element from the amount in your soda pop to its presence in laundry detergent and the amount of runoff affecting streams, rivers, lakes and waterways. An essential nutrient for plants, animals and humans, too much phosphorus in the water causes algae to grow faster than ecosystems can handle. Significant increases in algae harm water quality, food resources and habitats, and decrease the oxygen that fish and other aquatic life need to survive. Algal blooms are harmful because they produce elevated toxins and growth that can make people sick. Large growths of algae are called algal blooms, and they can severely reduce or eliminate oxygen in the water, leading to the death of large numbers of fish.

Yet as the story leaked out, we now know Brand had discovered an incredibly powerful element. He found his purpose in atomic number 15 or as we now know it ... P.

Make the most of your time

So what did you do during the downturn? Your time of isolation? Spend it in the basement? Reinvestment comes in the form of caring for your health too. Gardening and the physical aspects give you the exercise you need. During the pandemic there was debate about precautions and practices that needed to take place for the good of all. Exercise is no different. When you take care of your health and exercise, you are contributing to the overall good of everyone, not just yourself. You are better able to contribute to the well-being of others and reduce the cost and strain on general overall health care costs.

It all adds up to the reality that we were not created, not wired, to spend only 1% of our life exercising and certainly not sitting in a box with an artificial atmosphere. Live outdoors.

If an average life expectancy is 25,915 days (71 years), it is said an average human would spend 1% (or 259 days) exercising. 29.75% of their time (7,709 days) is spent sitting down. If that is true then more people need to garden. It is understood that an outdoor lifestyle with moderate physical activity is linked to longer life, and gardening is an easy way to accomplish both. If you garden, you're getting low-intensity physical activity and you tend to work routinely. Routinely being the keyword there. It doesn't have to look pretty. So Mom was right all along. She would kick us outside especially if we complained about being bored.

As a runner, I read a study with interest that pointed out arm swinging costs energy while running, but holding them steady takes even more energy. I would look rather silly running with my arms held steady. That's because arm swinging reduces the motion of the torso. Running a marathon can produce physical pain but when you finish it is an emotionally positive experience. Your sense of accomplishment can mitigate your memory of the tough stuff. If a painful activity produces outcomes of value, positive emotions result, and these emotions seem to help ensure that pain does not prevent us from doing it again.

There is no panacea for growing old, but gardening does appear to improve our quality of life. Let nature nurture you. The social benefits too can increase longevity. Areas around the world that have the highest ratio of centenarians to the general public population often have residents that maintain personal gardens. It can't be just a coincidence.

In early American history, family home life was, by today's standards, full, sprawling households. Odds are only one bathroom too ... outside. In the early 1800s three-quarters of American workers were farmers. Most of the other 25% worked in small family businesses, such as a dry goods store. A lot of labor was needed to run these entrepreneurial fledgling examples of American capitalism. And how do you staff this enterprise? With kids. Relatives. It was not uncommon for married couples to have seven, nine or more than ten children along with other relatives, even aging grandparents. In the same house.

In Japan they say that anybody who grows old healthfully needs an "ikigai" or reason for living. Gardening gives you that something to get up for every day. They combine that with "yuimaru" or a high level of social connectedness. I have found that on my radio show. People love the social interaction that a common interest like plants affords. It helps people feel grounded and connected. Eating more vegetables and plants will make you healthier. There is a simple truth. And gardeners are more likely to plant what they want to eat.

> *"I have found only two types of non-pharmaceutical "therapy" to be vitally important for patients with chronic neurological diseases: music and gardens."*
> *– Oliver Sacks, neurologist and author*

Exercise and time to let your mind wander is so important. A sedentary body or mind is like a plant locked in a dark closet. No matter how well the plant is fed or watered, it will decline and die without sunlight. The same seems to be true of a human body denied regular physical activity and mental stimulation. Like the plant's position, you would need to adjust your hebetude. If exercise were a drug they could market it as a wonder drug. Exercise involves and activates every organ of the body, including the brain. Take care of the three things gifted everyone ... your mind, your body, your spirit and be thankful for the gift given all of us. Forgiveness. Haven't been doing well lately? Remember it's never too late to start.

You might not be able to change your reality but you CAN change how you experience it.

Researchers have suggested you most appreciate life's experience and feel like you know your purpose best when you're around age 60. That's the age when people report feeling that there's the most meaning in their lives, and they have the least need to search for meaning. When a person's sense of meaning in life rises, so does their well-being. It's understanding your purpose that can help make you both physically and psychologically healthier.

You're among fronds

Life can be a storm when you're trying to figure it out. Storms are exciting. They also tax our reserves and can cause setbacks. As you seek your purpose there are times of sacrifice and times of endurance. A good example of a plant doing what needs to be done, including at times sacrifice, is the Royal Palm *Roystonea regia*. It is a tree that does what has to be done (you don't need to be a palm reader to see what is happening here). When it's time to endure it is able to bend without breaking. I have observed these palms in southern Florida. They have fronds that will break off from the crown of the tree before winds are strong enough to topple the trees. The fronds sacrifice for the long-term benefit of the tree as a whole. In a severe hurricane they sacrifice all leaves to ensure survival. This happened during Hurricane Andrew in 1992 with wind speeds of over 165 miles per hour.

The foliage plant industry in Dade County was devastated by hurricane Andrew in August, 1992. After the storm, many who worked in the plant industry were forced to leave the area because of insurmountable personal losses. The storm damaged or destroyed thousands of acres of nursery shade houses and greenhouses, and ornamental foliage nursery crops. Many plants not destroyed directly were damaged or died later as a result of desiccation due to lack of irrigation, and solar exposure due to lack of shade. Some plants that survived, but were abandoned in the field, grew at a 90-degree angle to the light and were called "Andrew survivors." In spite of tremendous adversity, a large share of Dade County's nursery firms rebuilt their facilities. Many plant growers moved aggressively to start new crops and resume business immediately.

Storms don't always come to disrupt our life. Sometimes they clear a path. Reset button.

I walked the fields a couple years after hurricane Andrew and witnessed the resilience of those who stayed. This mayhem originated with the evacuation orders given to people in the danger zone before the hurricane hit: no pets allowed in the shelters. Leave your pooch or kitty at home in the bathroom with plenty of food and water in the toilet and bathtub. Don't worry, they'll be okay. Thousands of owners did leave their pets, following the hurricane experts' advice. But when homes burst apart, the animals emerged to discover a world without walls, fences or masters.

Consider Hurricane Florence in September of 2018 in the Carolinas. Callery pear, cherry, and other typically spring flowering trees and shrubs started blooming in October. This was likely a stress response related to the hurricane. Late winter and spring flowering trees and shrubs generally begin developing flower buds for the next year as soon as they finish flowering in the summer. However, storm damage including broken limbs, lost leaves, and flooded roots can lead to stress which changes the plant hormone levels causing plants to bloom and produce leaves out of season. Badly damaged plants sometimes put their energy into reproduction to create a new generation before they die. Trees that have a stress-induced, out-of-season bloom will have diminished or even no spring bloom. If the trees are otherwise healthy, they will likely leaf out the following year, and there should be no long-term effect. They went through a season of disruption.

When something disrupts my plot significantly its a virtual hurricane. It's up to me to improve my plot. When I do, the surrounding neighborhood improves in value. The right plant in the right place thrives. If it's not the right place you have to change your plants. Hydrangeas are loved by everyone but if they are in the wrong place they can be annoying and frustrating. What elements of your environment produce negative results? Change it. Don't waste a crisis. Don't be in the wrong place accepting marginal performance. Time is finite. Environments are infinite. You can run out of time in the wrong environment.

Many people are worried they will be "outed" when others realize they are operating by the seat of their plants. Don't worry odds are they are too.

If it seems like everyone else has it all together and you're struggling to survive, examine your environment. You need reinforcement. Consider the Buttercup family Ranunculaceae. They have arctic hardy species associated with freshwater environments. Known as the snow buttercup, *R. nivalis*, a vibrant bright yellow make them obvious buttercups with glossy petals and copious stamens in the center. Snow buttercup, as its name suggests, grows near the edge of melting snow banks found throughout the entire Canadian Arctic.

> ***"The flower that follows the sun does so even on cloudy days."***
> *– Robert Leighton*

They, like some other plant species, track the sun across the sky from east to west. It is referred to as Heliotropism. The snow buttercup is a good example. By facing the sun, the flowers of the snow buttercup are able to collect heat from the sun. The radiant heat helps the pollination effort as insect pollinators are warmed and deliver pollen more effectively to other plants. It's like smiling at someone, they tend to reflect your warmth back to you. A bright warm smile is infectious ... a bright warm yellow flower in a cold world. The warmth also appears to help the pollen germinate after it is delivered to another flower. When sunflowers face the morning sun, bees preferentially land on those warm sides. Look on the bright side, if things are tough at the moment work on your surrounding environment. It's going to get better.

You need to be able to breathe. Respiration.

In nature, roots need oxygen, roots respire too! Even though roots are "buried" the substrate is to serve as a site for air exchange between the root zone and atmosphere. In other words, roots need oxygen like we do. Some plant roots need a higher air porosity than others, but, have no doubt ... roots need oxygen. They need a balance between moisture and drainage. If you feel like you're drowning you need some drainage just like your plants. I can spot a plant a mile away whose roots are drowning. You can see it on someone's face too. Breathe. Adapt like the tiny Lithops and Haworthias. And when you help others like the fenestrated foliage of a Philodendron, you've improved your plot in life.

Rick Vuyst

I wonder you can do me a favor
It could actually be a face saver
Before you chatter
Think. Before the latter
And spare me the clishmaclaver

Chapter Twelve
Teasel and the Dame's Rockets

> *"Ay' quoth my uncle Gloucester, small herbs have grace, great weeds do grow apace. And since methinks I would not grow so fast, because sweet flowers are slow and weeds make haste."*
>
> *– William Shakespeare*

I ALWAYS WANTED TO BE LEAD SINGER and a guitarist in a rock and roll band. It didn't have to originate in the UK or Seattle but I guess that would be a bonus. One with a one-hit wonder and 15 minutes of fame. The Billboard Top 100 through the ages is lined with one-hit wonders. As I run down the trail on a hot July night my mind wanders to what that would be like. I think the band would need to have an interesting name.

> *"One run can change your day.*
> *Many runs can change your life."*

I continued running down the trail looking at the tall, dark, spent, year-old seed heads of a multitude of Teasels while the new, ready-to-bloom Teasel were catching up in size. Already a year removed from the previous July I think how time flies. The bright yellow finches flitter in front of me from plant to plant intoxicated by the buffet of seed heads on 6 to 8 foot stems. After running this trail in June, lined with thousands of Dames Rockets in bloom, and in the heat of July with thousands of Teasels in bloom, I now know what I would name the band. *Teasel and the Dames Rockets*.

Maybe it was the 90-degree heat that caused my mind to wander. Maybe it was my disappointment. After 6 months of training to celebrate my 60th year on earth I was scheduled to run the Chicago Marathon in October. That July day I was running the trail, it became one of thousands of events canceled in 2020 due to a worldwide pandemic. I was disappointed but I understood. I would have to change my plans.

You won't cross the finish line if you don't have a desire to run the race.

We all have our moment in the sun. The Abbott World Marathon Majors is a series consisting of six of the largest and most renowned marathons in the world. The races take place in Tokyo, Boston, London, Berlin, Chicago and New York City. The suprachiasmatic nucleus in my brain reminded me that my clock is ticking at the age of 60, and preparation and opportunities to run marathons might not be there in the "long run." In the interim I would continue to run to stay fit and allow my mind the opportunity to wonder as I wander. That includes fantasizing about rock star status. Vivelo! Let's live everyday to the fullest.

Teasel and the Dame's Rockets

Common Teasel was imported from its native Europe into North America and is a plant with one of the best botanical names. *Dipsacus sylvestris* with common names like barber's brush, brushes and combs, or church broom. Its leaves are fused around the flowering stem, forming a cup that collects rainwater. Common teasel produces puckered leaves with scalloped edges in the form of a rosette during its first year of growth. The second year a 6 to 8 foot tall stem and prickly flower cone emerges. Dipsacus was derived from the Greek verb meaning "to be thirsty," which is in reference to the water collecting cup leaves. The common names card teasel and card thistle are in reference to the wire brush or card used to tease wool. Teasing is simply pulling the fibers of wool apart. Carding is smoothing the fibers out. Regardless, I'm sure the wool had it coming. Seeds of the teasel usually fall within 5 feet of the mother plant so you will see large clusters of them. I've watched goldfinches feeding on the thistle-like seeds, so I'm sure they aid in the distribution and propagation process. An average teasel plant produces over 3,000 seeds.

Dames Rocket also has a great botanical name, *Hesperis matronalis*. Common names are Dame's violet, mother of the evening and sweet rocket. Loved or reviled, it does have an evening fragrance. Hesperis means "of the evening" and matronalis "of matrons" referring to its perfume scent. Dame's rocket is an abundant seed producer. When the seed-bearing pods ripen, they pepper seed onto wildlife, allowing for extensive seed spreading. The plant infiltrates waterways, wetland margins, farm fence rows, ditches and tree lines, and colonizes expanses at the expense of native plants.

Dame's rocket has explosive growth patterns similar to its close relative in the mustard family, garlic mustard, also a prolific seeder. It also has allelopathic tendencies that prevents or reduces the growth of other plants similar to garlic mustard. Both Dame's Rocket and Garlic Mustard quickly form dense monocultures within a few years of colonization. Some call it a wolf in sheep's clothing, because Dame's Rocket is pretty at 55 mph along a roadside and may be confused for a native phlox. Phlox all have five-petal flowers where Dame's Rocket has four petals. As a prolific bloomer, each plant thus produces a copious amount of seed. It is very good at setting its footing in disturbed soils when the opportunity arises.

Most "weeds" are opportunists and produce abundant seed. Many have allelopathic chemical inhibition tendencies where one plant inhibits its neighbor due to the release of substances acting as germination or growth inhibitors. In 1832, Swiss botanist Alphos-Louis-Pierre-Pyramus DeCandolle speculated that noxious weeds may exude chemicals from their roots that inhibit the growth of other plants. Allelopathy. ***This toxic inhibition is just like negative attitudes. It drags everyone down with it and growth is stifled.***

Negativity is contagious

There it was. Innocent enough looking and pretty in mass in the hot summer sun with plentiful pinkish lavender hue blooms dotting the landscape. It has a dark side as a foreigner persona non grata crowding out the natives. A national menace it is the wicked weed of the west in the plain states. Spotted Knapweed. Spotted knapweed conducts chemical warfare on its neighbors. Spotted knapweed arrived in Victoria, British Columbia, in 1883 either as a contaminant in imported alfalfa or in soil used as ship ballast. Since then it has dug in across the United States and Canada. For now, sheep seem to be the answer as they, unlike other grazers, seem to be able to stomach spotted knapweed.

Weed need to talk

Idle talk, gossip, negativity are like weeds. They spread easily. They have to be rooted out and not reinforced. The Scottish have a great word for it: clishmaclaver. Idle talk, gossip, or empty chatter. Good breeds good. Bad breeds bad. The landscape, like people, thrive on positive momentum.

Without answers you need visionaries with positive intentions to move people forward. To cultivate possibility thinking.

Nothing stays the same. You are either moving forward or backward. The reason a vehicle's windshield is much larger than the rearview mirror is that we need to be looking forward and anticipating. The rearview is still important, the ability to look back for perspective. Though we may not care to admit it, what other people think about something can affect how we think about it. This is how critics become influential and why our parents' opinions about our life choices continue to matter, long after we've moved out. Negative opinions cause the greatest attitude shifts, like invasive weeds, not just from good to bad, but also from bad to worse.

There's a common saying that goes, "Don't believe everything you hear," and in today's digital age not everything you read. But sometimes, we have to remind ourselves not to believe everything we think. We establish a position, a thought, a belief, and then we dig in or "entrench" ourselves to defend the position to both ourselves and to others. Our thoughts sometimes can deceive us. Healthy interaction and discussion with others help you cultivate positions that are not polarizing but rather move the community actions forward together toward mutual benefit.

Weeding out negativity and generating positive momentum has to be done by encouraging others to join in. When you work together you stand apart. There is strength in numbers and drifts of flowers make an impact.

> *"To invent, you need a good imagination and a pile of junk."*
> *– Thomas A. Edison*

It was the age of enlightenment. What a time to be alive. Especially in the colonies or the "New World." I plant myself in that time and sense an air of discovery, questioning, development and invention while simultaneously not losing sight of caring for your neighbor, your fellow man. The lesson still applies. Even in the modern era today, work is a pilgrimage of purpose and understanding. Work has to make sense to the one engaged in it and have meaning to those benefitted. If it doesn't, well, it just doesn't work. It was something we were again reminded as we gained 2020 vision in 2020. Whether a revolution from a monarchy or a health crisis, necessity would be the mother of invention.

> *"As we enjoy the advantages from the inventions of others, we should be glad of an opportunity to serve others by any invention of ours; and this we should do freely and generously."*
>
> *– Ben Franklin*

Benjamin Franklin's inventions were practical and designed to make everyday life easier. He considered his inventions a gift to the public. In his autobiography he wrote: "As we enjoy the advantages from the inventions of others, we should be glad of an opportunity to serve others by any invention of ours; and this we should do freely and generously."

It was one of Ben Franklin's friends, Joseph Priestly, who engaged in experimentation for the general wellbeing of his fellow man. In the course of these experiments, Joseph Priestley made a significant and meaningful observation. A flame would go out when placed in a jar and the resident mouse would die. Both the flame and the rodent failed due to lack of air. Putting a green plant in the jar and exposing it to sunlight would "refresh" the air, permitting a flame to burn and the mouse to breathe. Priestley wrote, "the injury which is continually done to the mouse is in part at least, repaired by the vegetable creation." He had observed that plants release oxygen into the air, and he hypothesized on the process known to us as photosynthesis. You could say the end results were a validation of the importance of plants and that in his experimentation Priestly needed to change his plants, resulting in mouse-to-mouse resuscitation.

In the American colonies intellectual ferment sowed the seeds of revolution by the likes of Thomas Paine, Thomas Jefferson, Alexander Hamilton, Ben Franklin, James Madison, George Washington and Jared Eliot. Jared Eliot?

Jared Eliot was a wise and educated man, an American colonial minister, physician, agronomist and farmer who died before the seeds of revolution exploded in Lexington on April 19, 1775. Eliot attempted trade with other countries, but was unsuccessful before his death on April 22, 1763. By 1765 the Stamp Act was invoked by the British, and relations between the colonies and Britain by then were arduous and irreparable.

It is notable Mr. Eliot's death occurred on April 22, 1763. Ironically this is 207 years to the day before the first Earth Day, April 22, 1970. Earth Day founder Wisconsin Senator Gaylord Nelson came up with the idea for a national day to focus on the environment after witnessing the ravages of a massive oil spill in Santa Barbara, California, in 1969. Since then Earth Day is always observed on April 22. Eliot's death before both the fruition of the revolution and Earth Day prove he was a man ahead of his time with actions and thoughts characteristic of a later age.

Jared Eliot who was interested in soil mineral quality as an agronomist, wrote his first "essay" or book concerning land improvement for agricultural crops throughout the colonies. He wrote other subsequent "essays" to "set before the reader the way of mending our poor land and raising crops." Central to the method of raising crops in an efficient manner was his work on the development of a drill plow. One man and a team of oxen could efficiently plant straight rows of seeds well beyond the efforts of many sowing by hand.

Jared Eliot designed a plow cheaper and simpler than the one developed by English agricultural innovator Jethro Tull. Many would think of the 1960s rock band from England when hearing the name Jethro Tull. The connection of the English agricultural innovator to the band? None. At the time, booking agents would make up names for fledgling bands, finding their way without a name before a gig booked at a venue. The rock band *Jethro Tull* was using the name the first time a club manager liked their show enough to invite them back. They took it as a good omen and stuck with the historical name.

Instead of cultivating rock music, Jared Eliot was a man interested in the cultivation of minds. His problem with Jethro Tull was he made the concept too complicated and difficult to understand with words that were not "open and easy to understand." He set about to make both mechanical improvements to the plow as well as rhetorical improvements of the language used to explain it. A precursor to the owner's manual that most people don't read today when they buy something. He complained the Englishman had little regard to the reading capacity of the common farmer.

Years after the American Revolution we view those who fought in it with a nostalgic romanticism of citizens, farmers and laborers, young and old who picked up their muskets and fell in with their militia units to defend home, farm and community from invading Redcoats. Many were hardworking earthly people without the benefit of a formal education. Many soldiers were "unlearned" farmers as Eliot would describe them, just as the common Revolutionary soldier, but one thing is certain. We remain in their debt. Prior to the revolution it was Eliot who wanted a forum to disseminate practical knowledge freely and clearly to all regardless of their educational "status." He is famously quoted as saying,

> *"I have learned many useful things from the lowest of people, not only in rank but in understanding too."*

The quote to some could come across demeaning and condescending but Jared's heart I believe was in the right place. He understood with proper intentions you could influence positively the path or "row" of another. He inherited the attitude from both his father and grandfather who as missionaries and "clerical physicians" were interested in helping others, including teaching others proper hygiene and better living.

Bean there done that

It could be argued that one of the most impactful plants in the age of the enlightened human was not tobacco, corn or cotton but was the coffee plant. Tea was the most favored drink in the colonies until the colonists revolted against a heavy tax on tea imposed by King George III. The revolt, known as the Boston Tea Party, would forever change the American drinking preference to coffee. And if 2 cups of tea equal one cup of coffee for caffeine content, you could say we woke up to the tyranny of King George and his taxation without representation. Turmoil brought about change and change was coming.

> *"Coffee. The favorite drink of the civilized world."*
> *– Thomas Jefferson*

Coffee cultivation and trade was known by the 16th century in places like the Arabian Peninsula, Persia, Egypt, Syria, and Turkey. And coffee legend and lore can trace its heritage to the ancient coffee forests on the Ethiopian plateau. The legend is about a goat herder named Kaldi who first discovered the impact of the coffee bean from his goats. Goats of course will eat almost anything including poison ivy. Kaldi discovered caffeination when he noticed that after eating the berries from a certain tree, his goats became so energetic that they did not want to sleep at night. And they certainly were more talkative. It certainly made the monks he shared his berries with more alert through long hours of evening prayer. They made a drink of the berries, stayed awake during prayers and soon the rest was history. News of the energizing berries began to spread.

The coffee tree is a tropical evergreen shrub. Coffee comes from the seeds of a small tree with the dominant species being *Coffea arabica*. The average Arabica plant is a large bush with dark-green oval leaves. The fruits, or cherries, are rounded and mature in 7 to 9 months; they usually contain two flat seeds, the coffee beans. When only one bean develops it is called a peaberry.

European travelers in the 16th and 17th centuries brought back stories of an unusual dark black beverage. By the 17th century, coffee had made its way to Europe and was becoming popular across the continent.

In the mid-1600s, coffee was brought to New Amsterdam (also called New York) by the British. Tea was the favored drink in the New World until December of 1773, when the colonists revolted against a heavy tax on tea imposed by King George III by pitching 342 chests of tea into Griffin's Wharf in Boston, Massachusetts. The revolt, known as the Boston Tea Party, would forever change the American drinking preference to coffee. The revolt proved a boon to coffee houses in the colonies.

Across Europe and in the new world colonies, coffee houses were quickly becoming the epicenter of social activity, news, idea sharing and communication in the major cities. In England "penny universities" sprang up, because for the price of a penny you could purchase a cup of coffee and engage in stimulating conversation. Oh if they could see the vendor dispensing machines in rest stops along highways today.

Coffee began to replace the common breakfast drink of the time which was beer or other alcohol beverages. Those who drank coffee instead of alcohol began the day alert and energized and their work performance improved greatly. I'm sure at evaluation time the boss made note of the punctuality and improvement. Before the discovery of coffee, much of the world was intoxicated throughout the day. Water was too polluted to drink, so beer was the beverage of choice. What an advancement for civilization to begin the day alert instead of buzzed. New ideas were shared and industrialization benefited.

Missionaries and travelers, traders and colonists carried coffee seeds far and wide as an early version of coffee to go. Coffee trees were cultivated worldwide. Plantations were established in magnificent tropical forests and on rugged mountain highlands. By the end of the 18th century, coffee was a major and profitable export crop.

Coffee Grounds

The middle ground is not always a bad place. It often is where common sense dwells. Especially if you can handle two opposing views and still be able to function.

As we meet in coffee houses and drink the elixir of awareness it's up to us to sow the seeds of positivity. Though we may not care to admit it, what other people think about something can affect what we think about it. Negative opinions cause the greatest attitude shifts from good to bad to worse. It spreads abundantly because the environment is conducive to weed growth. Bare ground is not a natural condition. Something is going to grow there. Usually weeds. And just because it spreads doesn't make it good or grounded.

Negativity spreads fast ... positive attitudes are slower.

Cultivating positive thinking is quite similar to growing a garden or farming crops. It doesn't take much effort to grow weeds. These nettlesome participants in a garden or crop area grow without any help. They can quickly pop up and spread and once there can be hard to eradicate. The same holds true with our negative thoughts. It takes little effort to have negative thoughts; it takes considerable effort, however, to get rid of weeds and grow the plants you want. Getting rid of negative thoughts to start growing the positive ones takes work. Just as it's worth doing the hard work to rid your harvest of weeds, it's also worth the hard work it takes to rid your mind of negative thoughts. Try again. Failures are simply success in progress.

A road less traveled

As I run down the trail looking at the tall teasel, the blooming spotted knapweed and the aroma of dame's rocket in bloom, I think the trail of negativity is a path most really don't want to travel. It grows weeds and eventually turns into a copse or underbrush. Those who seek to run that trail later will have extra work to do. Excavation and clearing of the thicket needs to take place slowing everything down. Life on the road less traveled. The reality is you have to find your way, sometimes down a difficult path called experience. The path you choose and how you run it is optional. Like the Oakleys reminded me: it's not always what you **did** in life, but it's what you **didn't do** that creates regret so get out there and do it. As for *Teasel and the Dame's Rockets* we choose to rock on.

I walk through a stand of trees
We care as their natural trustees
I stand in their shade
A foliar parade
The path is a wooded reprise

Chapter Thirteen

They Don't Even Know I Xyst

IN 1980, PRESIDENT RONALD REAGAN implied that trees produce more air pollution than automobiles. This fueled a plethora of jokes about "killer trees" during an election cycle. In an election year, Reagan was lampooned by Democrats for claiming that a large percentage of air pollution was caused by plants and trees. Reagan aides later said the then-presidential candidate had been misquoted and was referring only to certain types of pollutants, not to all air pollution. Before we get out chainsaws, let's remember that trees give us the oxygen we breathe, and the candidate's words were taken out of context. They also provide shade, cooling and scrub many pollutants from the air. Maybe the 'whole trees causing pollution thing' was started by allergy sufferers and the trees proclivity for radial distribution of pollen in season.

> *"Trees cause more pollution than automobiles do."*
> *– Ronald Reagan*

It's not the trees' fault we're throwing NOx or oxides of nitrogen (especially as atmospheric pollutants produced during combustion) at them. Many times my friend Quercus (Oak) is blamed

I Need to Change My Plants

for the conundrum just like the former president. Isoprene is emitted from some plants, and it appears to have an adaptive role in protecting leaves from abiotic stress. In hot weather, trees release volatile organic hydrocarbons, including terpenes and isoprenes. In very hot weather, the production of these begins to accelerate. It's not clear to me why plants emit isoprenes and other gases, however, some people much smarter than me seem to think it protects photosynthesizing leaves from heat stress.

The haze hovering above the Blue Ridge Mountains or America's Great Smoky Mountains contains isoprene, reacting with other chemicals in the atmosphere to form particles. These particles give the haze its color. Float nitrogen oxides over a forest of isoprene emitting oaks, throw in some sunshine and heat and ozone levels will climb. The "smog" will be visible.

> Sylvan
> syl·van | \ ˈsil-vən \
> Consisting of or associated with woods; wooded.
> Pleasantly rural or pastoral.

Arbor Day was almost called Sylvan Day, which means "wooded." Several members of the Nebraska State Board of Agriculture favored it, but J. Sterling Morton, Arbor Day's founder, argued that sylvan refers only to forest trees and that the name Arbor Day was all inclusive, covering forest trees, backyard trees, rural and city trees and orchards. Sylvan would be a great name for a kid who loves nature. All of us are in some way sylvestral. And when the orchestral symbionce of leaf tissue collectively presents the grand finale known as autumn, the trees get a lot of attention and help fund the economic engine of communities blessed with natural vistas.

Xyst
A garden walk planted with trees

xyst[zist]
noun
(in an ancient Roman villa) a garden walk planted with trees.

Fresh air. Always a good thing, and we especially craved it during the 2020 pandemic. Over one hundred years ago it appears that health officials correctly assessed that fresh air would ward off airborne diseases and germs. When visiting older apartment buildings in New York City, you observe bulky radiators coated in layers of paint for steam radiant heat throughout the building. In winter the radiant steam heat warms the rooms to the point you need to take that sweater off and crack the window open even though it's January. Heat rises so the apartments above can get quite toasty. I now know why the Board of Health in New York City ordered that during the winter windows should remain open to provide ventilation during the pandemic of 1918 and 1919. Radiators and their radiant heat were designed to heat buildings with the windows open during cold weather. It was a "fresh air movement."

In 2020 one of the words that emerged was Cottagecore. The cottagecore aesthetic is a romanticized interpretation of rural life. Imagine idyllic country life, fresh air, cozy interiors, rolling fields, flower print, straw hats, homemade baked goods, growing plants, raising animals, and flowers. The trend was led by celebrities and influencers who had escaped pandemic-plagued cities for rural enclaves. A calming ethos, a pastoral existence complete with immaculate golden-brown lattice fresh-baked pies with their crust cooling on a kitchen counter and windows open with checkered curtains flapping in the breeze. Clothes are hung from a clothesline in the backyard dotted with large shade trees. Another world.

When you live in the city you miss the benefit of a fresh air forested walk. I "xyst" for moments like that. I love a walk through a wooded area any season of the year. In winter, when we are confined to our homes with closed windows, the refreshing saunter the woods can provide is rejuvenating. Forest synergy is real, and symbiosis is natural with plants. Nature gives us examples of beneficial mutualism versus polarizing adversarial parasitism relationships among plants. There is interaction between two different plants or trees living in close physical association, sometimes to the advantage or disadvantage of both and others. Healthy cooperation between living things produces a combined effect greater than the sum of their separate parts. A need for community. But they don't even know I xyst. I just benefit. It's like natural occurring mycorrhiza and its role as a beneficial fungus in a tree's rhizosphere, or root system. Mycorrhizae play important roles in plant nutrition, soil biology and soil chemistry. That's what's going on in the unseen root zone to the benefit of all. But what about the canopy of a tree?

Know your "limb-itations"

I have, from time to time while walking through a wooded area, noticed the uppermost branches of certain tree species that don't like to touch one another. Way up there in the tops of the trees they seem to be practicing social distancing?

This phenomenon known as crown shyness or canopy shyness is when branches in the crown do not touch branches from other trees, forming channel-like gaps in forest canopy. There are hypotheses that it occurs in order to reduce the spread of harmful insects. Some believe spacing naturally occurs so trees can optimize light exposure for the process of photosynthesis in both their leaves and leaves of foliage on the forest floor. Others believe trees understand they sway in the wind and in order to keep branches from breaking they keep a safe distance.

Whatever the natural reason, it is mostly accepted that crown shyness is an adaptive behavior. The most logical physiological explanation is that crown shyness is simply the plant or tree's natural shade avoidance response. Growing tips sensitive to light levels slow growing when nearing adjacent foliage due to the induced shade and competition for light. They become shy. Being the pun aficionado that I am I will apologize in advance for this one ... they know their "limb"-itations.

Trees collaborate

Do plants social distance well? Sentience is the ability to perceive one's environment, and experience sensations such as pain and suffering, or pleasure and comfort. Now that plant communication is widely accepted, another question comes to mind: why does it happen? As noted in the past, it seems all too altruistic in a natural survival of the fittest scenario. Some scientists have suggested that the more proper term is actually "plant eavesdropping" when adjacent plants merely pick up what's happening to the one being harmed and prepare in advance to protect themselves from the impending problem.

An Idiom with two meanings: "Tighter than the bark on a tree"

1. Those two are closer than bark on a tree or close as bark on a tree.
2. He's as tight as the bark on a tree. Meaning he is very frugal.

The canopy of the forest tells a story. So does the intricate network of intertwined roots at our feet. Some form of communication takes place between trees via their world wide web of roots to the social habits of the tips of their branches. The trees, just like people, apply adaptive behaviors to cope with the stressors of life. That we do it is no surprise. Why we do it is another story and varies from individual to individual. Our past and our potential does not have to define our story today. Like the trees of the forest, we can stand tall today where we are planted and own our story as a part of the overall canopy of community. Others will benefit from our stories if we are all "truly in this together."

Diversity is important

Ash trees such as green ash, *Fraxinus pennsylvanica*, and white ash, *Fraxinus americana*, have been devastated by the emerald ash borer in neighborhoods. I have seen some streets where at one time large Ash trees lined the street, creating an inviting canopy over the drive. In fall their bright yellow color made the community neighborhood a magical place. I miss that vibrant yellow in the autumn sunlight. In short order the trees died and were cut down, and the old neighborhood just does not feel the same anymore.

Emerald ash borer is an exotic beetle that was discovered in southeastern Michigan near Detroit in the summer of 2002. The adult beetles feed on ash foliage but cause little damage. It is the larvae that kill the trees, feeding on the inner bark and boring through their cambium tissue areas beneath the bark, disrupting the tree's ability to transport water and nutrients. Emerald ash borer arrived in the United States on wood-packing material carried in cargo ships or airplanes originating in its native Asia. Since its discovery, EAB has killed hundreds of millions of ash trees in North America. It has caused regulatory agencies and the USDA to enforce quarantines and administer fines to prevent potentially infested ash trees, logs or hardwood firewood from moving out of areas where EAB occurs. The cost to municipalities, property owners, nursery operators and forest products industries is hundreds of millions of dollars.

And then there are the Elm trees. Until Dutch Elm disease began to ravage the American landscape in the 1930s, the elm tree was as American as apple pie. Images of commons shaded by elms, white clapboard houses along elm-tree-lined streets, churches with elm trees in the courtyard, street side store fronts cooled by their shade were iconic in many American towns. Autumn memories of trick or treaters walking the neighborhood sidewalks under a canopy of elms filtering the moonlight through their branches. A row of equally spaced elms on both sides of a street created an impressive green tunnel of dappled shade. Many towns did not have high-rise buildings, so it was the elm-lined streets that became their visual embellishment. As trees grew large, they assumed a role of landmarks with monumental standing. An American Elm tree was planted during the administration of Teddy Roosevelt on the White House grounds somewhere between 1902 and 1906. During severe storms in 2006 the elm came down. Standing tall in our communities, they stood stately throughout our country along streets named Elm street and named in veneration with communities like Elmhurst, Illinois, Elm Grove, Wisconsin and New Haven, Connecticut considered the ''City of Elms.'' The bucolic effect was largely the result of the city's streets, which were lined with lofty, spreading American Elm trees just like the suburban streets were lined with White or Green Ash trees.

A Woody epidemic

The patriarchs of the purlieu, tree-lined streets welcome you home providing a grand entrance. Propinquity brought them together in one place for that wonderful neighborly feel. But neighborhoods lined with elm trees were too much of a good thing. The elm was never meant to be planted in monoculture clusters. A serious error in planting elms exclusively in lieu of other species, when Dutch Elm disease arrived, the effect was devastating. Dutch Elm disease, which was first described in Holland in 1919, spread like a wave through Europe in the 1920s and arrived in the United States in 1930 in logs imported for elm veneer. Contrary to what the name might suggest, Dutch Elm disease did not originate from the Netherlands. Most evidence suggests Dutch Elm disease originates from Asia, where many species of disease-resistant elms can also be found. The name actually reflects the fact that it was identified by Dutch phytopathologists Bea Schwarz and Christine Buisman. One infected tree meant an infected street, that street contaminates the next, moving on to the next neighborhood. The fungus was transported by flying bark beetles and by tree roots. The disease's causative agent *Ophiostoma ulmi* was introduced to the U.S. in the early 1930s. The American Elm, *Ulmus americana*, is extremely susceptible, and the disease killed hundreds of thousands of elms initially. Then came World War II and with the public's attention elsewhere, the woody epidemic flourished unchecked. Quarantine and sanitation procedures and efforts helped mitigate the spread until 1941 when war demands began to curtail them. Of the millions of elms in North America in 1930, over 75% had been lost by the 1980s.

If you peel the bark away from twigs which still retain yellow or browned leaves, the wood beneath the bark has dark streaks indicative of blockages in the water-conducting vessels of affected trees. The fungi that cause Dutch elm disease is transferred from infected trees to healthy elms by elm bark beetles, which carry spores of the fungi on their bodies and, in so doing, spread the disease. These beetles lay their eggs in infected trees. When the adult beetles emerge, they carry the fungus with them when they travel to healthy trees to feed on twigs and upper branches. From the feeding sites, the spores travel to the tree's water-conducting cells, or xylem. The xylem becomes plugged, causing the tree to wilt. Once the disease infects a tree, it may then spread to neighboring trees via interconnected roots. This occurs most commonly with elms in close proximity, which may have interconnected root systems. The disease is most easily detected during early summer when the leaves on an upper branch curl and turn gray-green or yellow and finally brown. This condition is known as flagging. In the mid 20th century the epochal classic elm was waving the white flag in surrender. Today, hybrids are being developed and grown resistant to Dutch elm disease in the hopes the tree can make a comeback in our neighborhoods.

Lesson learned

The saturation of a particular species in an environment can create havoc. Monocultures are an expensive lesson to learn when a problem spreads like wildfire. History repeats itself and we learn that diversity is important.

Other than dealing with nonindeginous-introduced diseases and insect infestations, do trees have a predetermined, predictable lifespan? And how long can trees live?

The best time to plant a tree was 20 years ago. The next best time is today.

We know in general, fast-growing weak-limbed species don't live as long as slower-growing trees. They live fast, cast some shade and die hard. Some trees just go down hard. But they have a lifespan. It was a sad day in December of 2017 when the historic Jackson Magnolia on the White House grounds had to be cut down after 19 decades. The tree, planted by Andrew Jackson, had far outlived the normal lifespan of its species when officials decided it would be unsafe to leave the tree standing. It even had survived the crash of a single-engine, two-seat Cessna airplane.

The iconic magnolia came to the White House as a seedling in 1829, following Jackson's victory in a nasty election campaign. Days after Jackson won the presidential race, his wife Rachel died. She had been ill for several years, but the vitriol of the campaign weakened her. Jackson, quick to blame his political opponents for his wife's demise, requested that a sprout from Rachel's favorite Magnolia tree, which stood on the couple's farm in Hermitage, Tennessee, be planted on the White House grounds. For nearly 200 years, the impressive magnolia tree cast its shade over the south façade of the White House, and, for a period of time, appeared in photos and on the back of $20 dollar bills.

Indeterminate growth

All plants die eventually. Most plants do have indeterminate growth, if conditions are right, they just keep growing with almost no limitations. There is no categorical and clear-cut lifespan for plants and trees. Sure, annuals live for just a growing season, produce seed and die. Unlike your pets, plants do not have a set age or size where they are considered old. Some plants do become elderly better than others due to genetics, environmental conditions and initial development. Without hurricanes, floods, fires and disease a tree can live a long, long time. As they get older, trees become more susceptible to disease, pests, and other perils, and inevitably these take their toll. As long as nature doesn't conspire against them they can continue to grow.

A difference between your household dog or cat and a plant is that plants have meristematic plant cells. They can change and divide many times. For as long as it survives, a plant is capable of indeterminate growth because it has perpetually embryonic tissues called meristems in its regions of growth. In essence, the cells within the meristematic tissues are what allow a plant to increase its length, girth and roots. This may explain why the Christmas cactus can live long enough to be passed along generation after generation as a family heirloom. A part of your inheritance, you didn't really want it, but feel guilty about discarding and breaking the cycle. Therein, long life is expected for a Christmas cactus or a fruitcake.

So no tree is immortal. Trees may have life spans, but they don't have fixed life spans like animals. It would be difficult for a human to live beyond 110 years but a tree can. Giant sequoias, Bristlecone pines, oaks and even bonsai trees can live to be hundreds of years old. Lifespans of trees, like those of all organisms, are limited. But they have a lot going for them. Apical meristems, located at the tips of roots and in the buds of shoots, supply cells for the plant to grow in length and become a seasoned regenerative citizen. The laws of physics do limit their height. When a tree cannot send enough water from the roots to the top layer of leaves it prevents adequate photosynthesis. Once they've reached maximum height, instead of growing taller, they grow wider. So a tree may not die of old age, but after a long enough time, consequence and circumstance dictate that it will die of some other cause.

Years of foliage leave a rich legacy on the woodland floor for those who follow. A foundation.

As a tree moves through its life stages, germination, whip, youth, prime of life, middle age, senior, twilight and death it is the gift that keeps giving. A set point for the seasons as they change. Don't underestimate the benefits of trees.

Trees do know how to *stick* together, better known as a forest. When you enter a bosk in winter, there are less olfactory distractions than in summer. In winter you can really sense the evergreen aroma, oils and fragrance. Ask anyone who has successfully cleared their head with a good walk in the woods.

Phytoncides, such as isoprene, alpha-pinene, and beta-pinene are in the forest air. Shinrin-yoku is Japanese for forest bathing. It is immersing oneself in nature, taking in the forest atmosphere as a gentle path to wellness. I could never have imagined something like this "xysted." Considered by some to be trendy, I think it's a great healing practice rooted in culture and history. A practice of taking in the forest atmosphere and breathing as a form of medicine. Scientific studies are now proving what we have always intuitively known, that nature can reduce stress levels in humans. Moods are improved and healing is accelerated.

Unplugging from our electronic devices and opening up the senses in a forest setting might be what you need to lower your blood pressure. Maybe a chance to be idle for a while and do nothing to enhance your creative juices. The Dutch have a great word for it called Niksen. My favorite word in this regard comes from Norway. Friluftsliv literally means 'free air life' in Norwegian. A spirit of friluftsliv is good for what ails us. We now know it is more than the peace of the forest, the unplugged feeling of fresh air and the exercise of a quiet hike through the trees. We now know that phytoncides, the essential oil produced by plants, has been credited with lowering stress and cortisol levels. Aromatic volatile oils are produced by trees like pine and hemlock as protective agents and are credited with the ability to lower your blood pressure. The phytoncides released by trees and plants into the surrounding atmosphere is to protect themselves from disease and harmful organisms. Inhaled phytoncides from a walk in the woods can last days in the human body.

We "xyst" together with the trees and an ethos all their own. Their beneficent boughs provide shade for the weary. We in turn give back to our fellow man by planting trees, under whose shade you do not expect to sit.

A bad smell suddenly arose
I picked up a scent with my nose
What is aromatic
To my nostrils dramatic
Compost takes time to decompose.

Chapter Fourteen
Plantasm

I COUNSELED A FRIEND WHO, IN A MO-ment of exasperation, said, "Things will never be normal again. Maybe this is the end of the world." Height, width, length and depth can sometimes be hard to measure when your perspective is at a point of frustration. Darkness clouds perspective. To console my friend I offered this prediction. "I can promise you we're going to get through this *and* things are going to **change**." It's not the first time in history things have looked bleak. Take heart, have faith, maintain perspective, and understand that change is inevitable.

The decade of 1810 to 1820 is one of the coldest on record. So cold that the summer of 1816 became known as the year without a summer. On June 6 of 1816 New England experienced snowfall of 10 inches. Freezing temperatures were experienced in Waltham Massachusetts in July of that year. Killing frosts in summer. In parts of North America and Europe the cold led to failed crops and near-famine conditions for millions of people. The North American economy, driven by arable farming, suffered in 1816 and the years beyond. Day after day of gloomy, dark, cold weather had many people fearing the world was facing its apocalyptic end. "Normal" ceased to exist. Mass migration seeking a better home, famine, disease, poverty, and civil unrest ensued.

Dark clouds upended seasonal customs and gelid caliginous conditions transformed customary existence, resulting in religious revivals as people tried to make sense of it all. I envision circuit riders or saddlebag preachers with flocks gathered around looking for answers. No one knew for sure what was happening. The circuit rider would preach and bring news including outdated newspapers. Families would feed him and he in turn would provide the message of salvation and "news of current events" to the answer-starved suffering citizenry. I can picture the horseback preacher climbing aboard a wagon and facing the people circled around.

> *"2 This is what the Lord says:*
>
> *"Do not learn the ways of the nations or be terrified by signs in the heavens, though the nations are terrified by them.*
>
> *3 For the practices of the peoples are worthless; they cut a tree out of the forest, and a craftsman shapes it with his chisel.*
>
> *4 They adorn it with silver and gold; they fasten it with hammer and nails so it will not totter.*
>
> *5 Like a scarecrow in a cucumber field, their idols cannot speak; they must be carried because they cannot walk.*
>
> *Do not fear them; they can do no harm nor can they do any good."*
>
> *– Jeremiah 10:2-5 (NIV)*

What we now know, that they didn't know then, was the biggest volcanic eruption in history, on the other side of the world had created all this environmental havoc. Mount Tambora exploded in Indonesia in April 1815. With it tons of dust, ash and sulfur dioxide were belched into the atmosphere changing the world's climate and dropping global temperatures precipitously. A huge and dense dust cloud had entered the atmosphere and was moving across much of the globe with ominous, far-reaching repercussions. They obviously got through it, but like any major cataclysmic event it sped the course of change. We would never be the same.

Lateral thinking

Being pruned changes the course of growth and that's OK. People, like plants, experience "pruning" in the form of setbacks, but, with both, the end result is forced lateral growth. Lateral: a side part of something, especially a shoot or branch growing out from the side of a stem. Pruning a plant back creates outward growth. Addition by subtraction. With a human a "pruning" set back forces outward growth beyond your comfort zone in the form of change. **Change is hard. Forced change is even harder.**

Our lives here on earth are finite. We have a limited amount of money, and time, and energy, and space. And we only get one chance to live our best life. How we decide to respond to setbacks and change has a profound impact on our future course from here on out. We didn't ask for it but sometimes change, as in pruning, is forced on us and we adapt with our response. At that point you have a decision to make. ***In fact, one of the most important decisions you'll ever make in life is deciding what is most important in life?*** Will you choose to grow from your experience?

For the everyday experiences and challenges I find life to be like a pendulum. It is suspended from a fixed point, and moves by the action of gravity and acquired momentum. Momentum is the key. It takes concentrated effort to create the momentum. Don't get bogged down in the failures; celebrate the successes, because ***Things aren't as bad as they seem and things aren't as good as they seem.***

The past can hurt. But from the way I see it, you can either run from it, or learn from it for the better. Even the simple squirrel digs in and instinctively responds to a brutal winter. During the gray squirrel's fall caching season, when the critters bury acorns, nuts and seeds in hundreds of scattered caches to serve as emergency winter larders, a typical squirrel shows a 15-percent increase in the size of its hippocampus, the memory and emotion center of the brain compared to the rest of the year. Coincidence or a natural built-in response? I think they rub the acorns on the side of their head to find the familiar scent later when hungry and wondering where the stash is buried. We can all find ways to creatively respond to a winter of discontent.

> **I need to change my plants:** When you change your attitude from "I am worried" to "I'm seeking answers" you are digging deep.

A Phantasm:
"A ghost or figment of the imagination"

I once lived on a property that I fully landscaped from scratch. I started to develop the landscape even before the home was fully built. With just a basement and some stud walls the landscape was going in faster than the house itself. I was excited, anxious, and could envision the end result. I would work alone, planting and developing the landscape often in the evening hours well after dark under the light of the moon. I did so much digging I developed what I call "Planter" fasciitis. If fasciitis is inflammation, then this "planter" and his muscles were sore due to all the digging. I worked hard, just me and a shovel. Or was it just me and my shovel? Did I have company?

When landscaping by the moon "after hours" and in the dark the shadows can play tricks on your mind. Things move, tools disappear and there are sounds. I know for a fact that upon occasion I heard voices. I sensed and heard foliage that would rustle even though the air was calm. Granted, I was working long days and was tired. But a large wood sculpture gifted to me from a friend, carved with a chainsaw, moved from its location. Not a "figleaf" of my imagination, the 6-foot sculpture was facing a different direction than I had placed it. It takes light to make a stationary object's shadow move. But for the object itself to shift position was peculiar and didn't make sense.

With the help of the local historical society, I did some research on the history of the land in that area. Previously the area was farmed and a number of adjacent corn fields still existed surrounding the new homes being built. The area, in the 1800s, was wooded with bears and wolves roaming the property. I found that in that area was a sawmill in the mid 1800s and that tragic mishaps had occurred there. That really got my mind wandering.

Once the home was complete and we had moved in, I invited friends for a party. After dinner in a candlelit, darkened room for effect overlooking the landscaped area, I recounted the area's history and my experience with the "ghosts." The laughter and guffaws at my expense for my perceived encounter, I'm sure were fueled by more than a few adult beverages and the atmosphere. But to this day my paranormal experience for me was real and I stand by the phantasm.

A Plantasm. A dream, a verdure vision, a "figleaf" of your imagination.

At least my zeal for the development of that landscape and the plant material placed there was real. I had a vision for what it would look like long before the plants had developed in size. I included favorites like Harry Lauder's Walking Stick, Dawn Redwood and Weeping Larch. I call that fanaticism and zest for plants and their arrangement a "Plantasm." For the enthusiastic about plants, a "plantasm" is the thought of a new plant or bargain frondescence arranged into a resplendent setting. Let me redefine the word.

> Plantasm. A dream, a verdure vision, a "figleaf" of your imagination.

Research has shown that gardeners buy thousands of plants over the course of their lifetime without having any idea where they'll put them once they get home. They do the walk. A shovel in one hand and a plant in the other looking for a place to put it. But a plantasm? That takes things to a whole other level.

An olfactory hallucination is called a phantosmia and causes you to detect smells that aren't really present in your environment. The odors detected in phantosmia vary from person to person and may be putrid or pleasant. How many times have you said to another, "do you smell that?" During 2020 temporary loss of smell known as anosmia, was a symptom and one of the earliest and most commonly reported indicators of the COVID-19 virus. In phantosmia the "phantom" smell may seem to always be present or it may come and go. Some refer to it as POP or Phantom Odor Perception, and over 5 percent of people over the age of 40 may experience it. The sensation can even vary from one nostril to the other. If you've experienced phantosmia and it's sticking around, I hope for your sake it was a pleasant aroma.

Plantosmia

I like to think that memories of aromas and scents whether real or conceived in the garden could be called "Plantosmia." Fragrance is an elusive quality that is high on the list for many people as a reason to garden. Years ago when good hygiene and bathing were not as common as today, flowers would be used to mask the less-than-pleasant aroma of the individual carrying them. They called them nosegays. The term nosegay was first used during the 15th century, and was a combination of the word nose and gay, with the word gay meaning ornament. The perfume of flowers sticks with you and is imprinted on your brain.

I can imagine aromas in my mind especially during the long cold mid-winter months. I dream of scents redolent of herbs like basil or lavender on a hot summer day. The balm of Monarda, the spice of Viburnum or Clethra when in bloom, the aura of Agastache as the bees and sphinx moths dance around their blossoms seemingly intoxicated. The perfume of Roses and the incense of Heliotrope on a hot summer day. These aromas are a part of you and embedded on your brain for recall on demand, even in the dead of winter.

Plantosmia can fill a functional role too. This is evident when taking a ride through farmlands and observing older homes or abandoned farm properties. I don't think it's my imagination that you see aged lilacs in bloom, near the old home as well as along the back of the property. I'll have to test my theory with some old timers, but I think they used them next to outhouses before indoor plumbing. When it was time to move the outhouse because the malodorous mess was overcoming, they would leave the lilac in place. A new lilac would be strategically placed next to the outhouse in its new location and the process again would commence. The lilac mitigated the fetor of the facility and provided some privacy screening to boot. Turns out the lilacs were more functional than decorative as landscaping; a century ago was not what it is today.

Maybe Lilacs should come standard with portable toilets today. You might hesitate using a "porta-john" but when nature calls a lilac would certainly change how you experience it. When visiting the Seattle area I noticed they call them Honey Buckets. It proves that with portable sanitation life is what you make it. Even if it's a figment of your imagination, your attitude can make the difference in how you experience everyday life. Whether functional or the sweet smell of success may your phantosmia be "phantastic."

Rick Vuyst

Confined to a house
Trying not to grouse
They're feeling captive
Trying to be adaptive
Then we come along and douse

Chapter Fifteen
Under House Arrest

MY PARENTS USE A WORD THAT ENcompasses the heart of Dutch culture. The Dutch tend to love anything that is "**gezellig.**" It is a word that cannot be easily translated to English. It's more of a feeling than it is a word. It's a mix of cozy and nice, comfortable and enjoyable, gregarious and quaint, warm and friendly all rolled up into one word. It's the cherry on the top of an ice cream sundae.

Well isn't this gezellig.

You have to practice the pronunciation to get it right. A gutteral "gha" with a "zell" wrapped up with a "lich" at the end that sounds like you're clearing your throat. Gha-zell-ich. At least that's how I learned it. And stay away from a place that is ongezellig. "I don't like going over there, it's just so ongezellig." Gezelligheid is a desired and respected condition the Dutch love, and, if you have it in your home, all's right with the world. Gezellig is an atmosphere you know and recognize when you feel it.

During a pandemic you are confined to home. It's a lock down. Just like our house plants we all needed a quarter turn, to see the light, a change of scenery. At times it wasn't gezellig, it was gloomy. The walls close in on you. Once again it was vegetation to the rescue! Houseplants can change the entire atmosphere, environment, mood and improve the air quality to boot. When humans were forced to stay-at-home, work from home, quarantine and distance from other humans with pandemic mitigation techniques in place, houseplants, already popular and embraced by many, once again saw rock star status. It was comforting and reassuring. With your maidenhair fern you were among fronds.

The resurgence of interest in indoor plants is led by the Millennial generation, those born between 1981 and 1996. If it is true that the now famous Millennial generation is more into "experiences" than things or consumption, then it only goes to reason they were driving a resurgence in plant interest. I had 3 Millennial kids and watched them grow up. I would remind them that when I was a kid we didn't have wood chips or padding in the playground. The swing, slide and monkey bars were above asphalt. We didn't have plastic slides, we had steel and metal slides that on a hot August day would be hotter than a pancake griddle and burn your backside. These are my "experiences" and I share them, which is usually followed by an eyeroll.

I love to watch the connection made between people and plants. When people purchase a plant I see some people hold it with 2 hands ... not by the lip of the pot, not by the stem but with 2 hands cupped under the plant. A nurturing hold from the start and a blossoming relationship has begun. They are their plant "babies." No diapers. Plants don't poop. Plants don't cry. They do throw up via guttation but it's not nearly as dramatic or smelly. They don't drink or eat much. You have to change a kid's pants, but with vegetation you CAN change your plants as often or as little as you want. You can talk to them but they won't talk back to you. You can show them off to friends. Post your nurturing prowess in social media. These are new plant parents. Plant parents or helicopter parents who touch, move and water their plants everyday. Your baby is beautiful. And the plants certainly aren't as messy or demanding as a pet. Just ask Gary Dahl the

1970s inventor who became a millionaire selling ordinary rocks after listening to friends complaining about having to care for actual pets. He sold 1.5 million rocks at $4 each to people searching for companionship in a 6-month fad during the Christmas season of 1975.

There is a national take your houseplant for a walk day commemorated each summer and why not? If they have to be cooped up inside they should get a chance for some fresh air too. Extra light and air and a chance to bond with your plants. You're a proud plant owner, so why not show them off a little bit. As part of the "new plant culture" I noticed taking plant walks being promoted complete with carrying cases and strollers. Their approach is that there are more plants under "house arrest," withering and sickened by being forced indoors and airing out your plants is "the responsible thing to do." There is no demographic for plant lovers. No age group, ethnic culture or gender preference. Plants are like good food. They feed the soul.

Sometimes you really need to just get out of the house. Stress relief. The dissidents challenge the establishment. If the authorities (that's you) force confinement of a plant they may challenge the establishment. Then trouble starts hanging around and bugs drip sticky residue on your floors, carpet and upholstery. If they don't want to be there things will go downhill fast. Think about it, even your front lawn naturally relieves stress through a process called guttation. Leaf blades or plants for that matter in summer under night time conditions of high humidity, cool air and warm soil have root pressure that can move water to the leaves. Since the stomata are closed at night, transpiration can not remove water from the leaf as it does during the day. The pressure builds and hydathodes, located on leaf margins near the ends of tiny veins, exude droplets of water to relieve the pressure.

I Need to Change My Plants

Only dead fish go with the flow.

Are you experiencing sickened and wilting plants? You may be experiencing root rot. It's a disease called pythium caused by overly wet soil and growing conditions. This soilborne pathogen is one of the main causes of root and basal stem rot. Pythium spores are good swimmers and move freely in wet soil affecting the root tips first. Soon it colonizes the root systems resulting in root loss. As a result, your plants will yellow, wilt, foliage will drop and the plant will slowly die. As a reaction we see the wilting plant and run for the watering can exacerbating the problem. Eventually the plant is killed by kindness. Hold off on that water, only dead fish go with the flow. Even a walk in the park isn't going to fix the stress that plant is under. Check frequently but water less. A lack of light and overwatering has been the demise of many plants under house arrest.

Forgive me I'm only humid

Humidity doesn't bother me. I like hot weather. Forgive me I'm only humid. I'm just like a Boston Fern. The sword fern *Nephrolepis exaltata* is known as "Boston" because a pioneering Florida nurseryman years ago shared them with a friend in Cambridge, Massachusetts where they were propagated by a local distributor. The ferns are notorious for wanting high levels of humidity and if they don't get it they have a bad hair day excessively dropping leaves and making a mess. They like hanging out on the front porch but are generally not used in interior landscaping for that reason. Summer air conditioning and winter heating is not conducive to a humid environment. Ficus, Palms, Schefflera and many other tropical region plants benefit from high humidity, because it reduces transpiration or water loss, browning of the edges of foliage and can discourage spider mites who love it dry. They let you know when they're not happy. Some plants are acclimated to dry arid air with little humidity. Generally these plants like succulents have thick waxy leaves and other adaptations for water retention, not the paper thin leaves of a fern. In summer I like to put them under an awning for some stay-cation time in the warm, humid air. Make sure they have some protection from wind and direct sunlight. And, if previous to summer they've been acclimating to your indoor setting, taking them into the direct sun will burn them just like you would by spending a June day on the beach after having been homebound all winter.

If you are asked by a friend to help with a failing or suffering plant, it's a real opportunity. You see in this world there are things that give people a feeling of power. Money, investments, exotic vacations, a fancy car, holding office, property, social status ... but we have learned, my friends, that nothing gives people the feeling of power more than...

Bringing a plant back to life from the brink of death.

Some house plants tend to live long enough to be passed down from generation to generation. If Grandma gifts you an heirloom plant there is a lot of pressure to keep it alive.

- Christmas Cactus (Schlumbergera)
- Jade Plants (Crassula)

I have been told that for 3% of people who buy a plant it dies the same day. That doesn't seem possible. I do know that browning of leaf tips and slow decline of a houseplant is a frustration for many people. I am convinced, aside from the light factor, that the watering issue is the struggle that results in the decline of the plant more times than not.

In lieu of knowing when and how to water, the indecision causes us to water small amounts often, such as daily, instead of deep watering when needed. We move from short-term solution

I Need to Change My Plants

to short-term solution, but never get to the true root of the problem. It's a metaphor for life when we trade what we want most for what we want in the moment. Don't be a "I can't figure it out so I'll water it often but just a little bit" person. What you will get is soil and roots where the upper portion is wet and drowning and the lower portion is dry as dust. And we wonder why the tips of the foliage are turning brown? It is true that a good, safe approach in life is to never test the depth of the water with both feet. However your fledgling foliage is suffering because the top half of the soil media is wet but the bottom half is dry.

In root-bound plants the water runs along the dense root mass at the top and down the sides of the pot and the dry contracted soil. Another good life analogy: When opportunity dries up, you contract and have to do something about it. Dry soil contracts from the side of the pot and moisture runs down the sides. Both you and your plant are missing out, because the core or center is not nourished or hydrated. You might look good on the outside but you're dying on the inside. Slowly but surely it starts to show. On plants "scars tell stories" and in many ways people are the same way. Those are lessons learned by experience.

Here's the thing. The bottom line: the suction pressure that exists within the water-conducting cells arises from the evaporation of water molecules from the leaves. Each water molecule has both positive and negative electrically charged parts. The main driving force of water uptake from the roots and transport up into a plant is transpiration of water from leaves. Transpiration is the process of water evaporation through specialized openings in the leaves, called stomates. It's almost as though the process defies gravity. If the plant is not transpiring due to cool temperatures or lack of light, the "suction" doesn't take place. As you pour more water on the soil and roots, they begin to rot. Don't panic, if an indoor plant needs water and starts to "flag" you have much more time to react than the plant that is outdoors in the wind, sun and exposed environment.

For many people I have been able to solve the mystery of watering a captive houseplant by employing the help of a cachepot. A cachepot is just a decorative container that holds a potted houseplant. Think of it as a pot inside a pot. The cachepot does not have drainage holes and holds the growing pot with drainage holes inside its walls. Margin for error is now improved and you can slide the growing pot out to observe and maintain the plant. When you pull the interior pot you can learn by the weight of the plant and the saturation level of the growing media. Mister bottles of water are not the solution. Do you mist your face when you're thirsty? Of course not. Mister bottles are like a pistol grip nozzle on a hose, good for watering a car or cleaning the patio furniture but not effective for landscape plants.

Maybe a ZZ plant, *Zamioculcas zamiifolia*, native to Africa, is for you. You may have to water it only 9 to 12 times a year. That's why some people call it a Bachelor plant. The closest thing you can find to plastic in a living plant. The plant can truly handle indecisive drought or neglect.

Consider the weeping fig or Ficus; this is a plant that sheds copious amounts of foliage when stressed. Who can blame it, with stressful transitions in its life in a short time. It is potted and grows in the field in a balmy paradise southerly location, is loaded on a truck pointing north, sold in a store environment, loaded in a car and finally placed in a home where the light can significantly vary from season to season and the air can be conditioned cold or heated dry. The plant does what it has to do. It is going to shed some foliage while it acclimates, sometimes as much as fifty percent of the foliage can shed when it decides to pout. Get out the vacuum cleaner. You're about to get a lesson in "modification." When we see that we run for the watering can and over water the plant. Soon it's over.

For both plants and people acclimatization commonly requires modification of activity. The adaptive changes permit us to handle seasonal variation and, on occasion, to move in

I Need to Change My Plants

> **I need to change my plants:** When you change your attitude from "I wish" to "It's time to plant" you're cultivating.

wholly new environments. The ability to become acclimatized differs greatly among species of plants and human individuals. Some are quite versatile in this ability, whereas others are narrowly restricted. The key word here is "modification." Are you up for it? Modification is a big word for change. I need to change my plants.

Let me shed some light on this

1. With houseplants "low light" doesn't mean a totally dark room. Some people have unrealistic expectations for plants ... you can't be in the dark all the time.

2. Most houseplants do not like direct blistering hot sunlight magnified through the glass.

3. That is why "bright indirect" light is the best choice for a houseplant in the home.

4. If the plants start to stretch and get leggy, it's a good sign they are not getting enough light.

5. If artificial light is the only option, then locate the plants as close to the light source as reasonable.

You can do this. And it's OK to be transparent and vulnerable when things go wrong. A lady in California was willing to do just that in the spring of 2020 when she had 6,000 shares and about as many comments on a social media post when realizing and admitting she had been watering a fake succulent for 2 years. She only realized it was fake when she went to repot it and discovered it was plastic with no roots. She said, "I feel like I have been living a lie."

Let me put it this way. When you're "barn blind" you think all the animals in your barn are better than they really are. That's the beauty of your plants. It really doesn't matter what anyone else thinks ... they're YOUR plants.

You CAN kill a Cactus

People use self deprecating one liners to lower expectations going into something. It gives them comfort to expect the worst at the outset so there is little disappointment when it happens. How many times have I heard the line "I killed a cactus?" Well if we're going down that road let me show you how.

This is how you kill a houseplant (the natives are restless):

- Keep them isolated with no humidity. Clustering is a great way to keep houseplants happy. They benefit each other when clustered. Strength in numbers. We're in this together. This is especially true with ferns. They need to know they are among fronds.

- Put your plant where it looks nice instead of near the correct light source.

- Leave it in your car or the garage

- Cold drafts (we're not talking about your favorite brew on tap my friends)

- Dry air. At a minimum dust the foliage occasionally which improves on available light to the plant

- Air conditioning. Some homes are air tight. A healthy home breathes. Open some windows!

- No drainage hole.

- Water your plant according to a schedule that suits you instead of when the plant needs it.

I Need to Change My Plants

- Poor quality potting soil mix.
- Don't inspect the plant for bugs. Aphids, mealybugs, mites will sneak up on you fast without warning.
- Give it the silent treatment. Talking to your plants is healthy ... for you. Sure the plant enjoys the carbon dioxide while it's improving your indoor air, but talking to your plants builds YOUR relationship skills. It's when they start talking back that you're in trouble.
- Don't over fertilize. Fertilizer makes plants work. With a houseplant the nutrients don't leach through like they do with outdoor plants. You don't want to make them work harder, just thrive.
- Go on vacation.
- Move.

It's OK if you kill a plant occasionally. If you haven't killed any plants you're not trying hard enough. And I realized this past year I'm a lot like plants. I started off as a green shoot, then grew into maturity trying to stay grounded. Eventually I'll decline and wait for the final harvest. This metaphor was used effectively by Shakespeare as he described the autumn and then the winter of man's lifespan, the pale ashes and dying embers of a fading fire. A little too dramatic? OK, I guess I'll water my plants. As stated so eloquently in Ecclesiastes, for everything there is a season, a time to live and a time to die, a time to plant and a time to harvest.

Rick Vuyst

Natural order and guarantee
The weight of gravity
The science consistent
The cycle persistent
The apple doesn't fall far from the tree

Chapter Sixteen
A Joule in My Crown

WHEN I WAS 15 YEARS OLD I GOT a job at a drive up and order restaurant with car hop service delivering food trays that hang on your partially opened window. The place was called Dog n Suds. The roadside sign had a goofy looking caricature canine holding a frothy mug of root beer. Dog n Suds was a midwestern chain of hot dog and root beer drive-in style eateries, featuring in-car carhop service. There was widespread popularity of drive-ins during the 1950s and 1960s which carried over into the 70s when I was employed as a teen.

The Apple doesn't fall far from the tree

Put teens on roller skates carrying both cash and heavy trays of food and big frosty mugs of root beer to curbside-parked cars to hang them precariously on a half-opened window and you ask yourself, what could go wrong? I remember an order where a customer wanted a "half burger" which didn't make sense to me. Not realizing they meant "halved" as in cut in half, I made the burger and sent out a half. As a growing 15-year-old boy I ate the other half. That didn't go down well as the customer returned asking where was the rest of their burger? That got me in a pickle and I certainly didn't get a "patty" on the back for that effort.

During peak demand I would be grilling multiple burgers and lining the buns out on wrap paper to prepare the condiments. When applying the ketchup or mustard I added that extra touch by "painting" smiley faces with the condiments. Squirts of mustard or ketchup with a sunny disposition. Pickles for eyes and a slice of onion as a smile. This didn't put a smile on my boss's face. He demonstrated the time is money approach. We aim the condiments in the general direction hoping some of it hits the target. Wrap it up and "order up!" I was just doing what my Dad would do when making burgers and I figured the condiment smiles were an added service touch. The apple doesn't fall far from the tree.

The gravity of the situation

Ancient proverbs say *"Der Apffel fällt nicht weit vom Baum"* or the apple doesn't fall far from the tree. The first recorded use of the phrase in the USA was by Ralph Waldo Emerson in 1839. Scattered around the bottom of an apple tree is the fruit it produces. When it drops to the ground it remains close to the tree it came from. This natural occurrence is a metaphor for traits and characteristics you inherited from your parents. Anyhow, the proverb is old and has hung around this long so it must be true. Regardless, apples were on my mind one day when I decided rappelling off a tall building would be a fun thing to try.

I took one of the elevators to the top of a building listed at 406 feet tall. At the top I was given training on ropes, a harness and taught the art of rappelling from some experienced professionals. I practiced at the top, leaning in the harness and learning to trust the rope. I tested my febrile imagination of relying on a rope for life and limb. When practice was complete I was ready to begin my descent. I was given a helmet that looked like something between a hockey helmet and bike helmet. I looked over the edge 406 feet down to the sidewalk wondering how the helmet was going to make a difference if something went wrong. I figured the helmet was a marketing ploy because pictures would be taken as I worked my way down the facade looking up. The company that did the training had their logo strategically emblazoned on the helmet. As you prepare to scale down the edifice, people gather with their phone cameras at the top and at ground level prepared to document the exploit of gravitational forces at your expense.

I step up to the parapet at the edge of the roof and the ropes are clipped to my harness. I place my right leg over the parapet and instantly a tingling sensation rushes all through my body. You're about to flip your left leg over the parapet and commit to going over the edge. A deep breath and another look to the pavement below. The people below look very small as they look up squinting waiting for the moment of truth. Would I do it? I shouldn't have looked down. It caused me to reflect on the laws of gravity.

It is at that point of going over the edge my thoughts turned to Sir Issac Newton the "inventor of gravity" when plunked on the head by an apple falling from a tree. Using his calculations on the laws of gravity I determined that from a 406-foot perch at the top of the building and my weight of 165 lbs, if the rope or harness failed I would reach the sidewalk below in exactly 5.01 seconds at a speed of 110 miles per hour. Utilizing a digital tool on my phone never available to the brilliant Issac Newton called "the splat calculator", I was able to measure the "joules" or force of impact if I were to hit the pavement below as applesauce.

A joule in my crown

One joule of force is equivalent to an apple dropped from 1 meter (3.28 feet) when it hits the ground. My joule force based on gravitational calculations, factoring building height and my weight, would be 90,405 joules. I thought *wow I'll go out with a bang having 5.01 seconds to think about it.* I had also heard that one Newton is 0.225 pounds and a typical apple's weight, dependent upon the species, size and water content is about 0.33 pounds. With a deep breath to clear my head of these thoughts I think I believe in the concept of gravity and the final destination is down whether by rope or elevator. With one leg already over the parapet and people above and below awaiting my next move, this was no time for second thoughts. I bolster myself by thinking *some people believe a fallen apple that inspired Sir Isaac Newton's ideas about gravity was simply a fabricated story.*

At this point wearing the operating room covers for my shoes you push off the glass and release hoping to create a rhythmic descent roughly a floor at a time. It actually went quite well and I was humored by the thought that people on the other side of the mirrored glass were watching me floor by floor. I was able to develop a rhythm until I was about ¾ of the way down the face of the building and at around 100 feet. That's when I discovered the need for the helmet. With 300 feet of rope "slack" above you, you suddenly recognize the crosswinds and breeze that are more than happy to rotate your position when pushing off the glass. The feeling of rotation bouncing you onto your back instead of your feet is not a good feeling. You have less control. The last 100 feet were less graceful than the first 300. Keep going. Robert Frost said it well. "The best way out of something is through it." Not around it, not under or over, not sidestepping ... but through it. I learned from NASA astronaut Jerry Linenger when I met him that "when you have passion for something barriers fall;" that if you stick your neck out there is not losing only learning. You go through it. So the first thing I did when reaching the ground was to kiss it. A good standing is not overrated.

Look down not up

The botanical application to all this storytelling is to first look down not up. I have an arborist friend who always tells me that when there are problems with your tree "look down **first**" not up. When troubles crop up, your grounding, your preparedness, your roots, your foundation, your experience become visually evident above the soil line. I thought *wow*! This applies to people too. A poignant perspective in times of trouble. I saw it time after time during the crisis of 2020 with people. I saw friends become enemies and enemies become friends. I saw how crisis, troubles, questions, instability reveal the true character of individuals. I have seen that same analogy with plants for years. When we start seeing sickly foliage, wilting foliage, anemic foliage, we start by looking at the foundation. The soil. Dirt is as basic and real as gravity. Are you well grounded? If not, for a tree it will become evident in the canopy. For a person it will become evident in your disposition. If things in general are looking up you can often "mask" unresolved problems and get away with it. But when the pressure is on and troubled seasons come along, how well you stand and how you react will depend on your roots. The apple doesn't fall far from the tree.

Gravity is as natural and basic as dirt.
Soil is a natural resource!

Soil is a mixture of minerals, dead and living organisms, organic material, air, and water. The interaction of these components along with weather conditions and the seasons makes soil one of the earth's most important natural resources. With soils there is some degree of physical, biological and even chemical weathering that takes place so even though it appears stationary it is technically dynamic. We just don't think about it because formation usually occurs at very slow rates unless we are physically amending the soil. "Parent" existing soils are limited natural resources. They are considered renewable because they are constantly forming.

Soils are made of layers, or horizons. Put the horizons together, and they form a soil profile. This was very evident to me as I observed the erosion along the Lake Michigan shoreline in 2019 and 2020. The layers are easy to see when exposed. Like a story, each layer tells a tale about the life of a soil. Soil just like people change with age. And just like with plants or animals there are soil classifications and a taxonomy system. A "soil order." Most people don't realize this. The soil orders all end in "sol" which is derived from the Latin word "*solum*" meaning soil or ground.

Some examples are:

- Gelisols are soils that are permanently frozen (contain "permafrost") or contain evidence of permafrost near the soil surface.
- Histosols are mainly composed of organic material in their upper portion.
- Vertisols are clay-rich soils that contain a type of "expansive" clay that shrinks and swells dramatically. These soils therefore shrink as they dry and swell when they become wet.
- Mollisols are prairie or grassland soils that have a dark-colored surface horizon. They are highly fertile and rich in chemical "bases" such as calcium and magnesium.
- Oxisols are soils of tropical and subtropical regions

I'm having dirty thoughts.

There was a run on soil amendments, potting soils and topsoil during the pandemic in the spring of 2020. There was a palpable ostensible desire to put your hands in the dirt. But what makes soil, soil? And aside from the utilitarian foundational components of it being a surface where we place our steps or its ability to support plant life, what was the draw? It is something I call "CAST." Soil is a supporting "cast" for the drama taking place all around us. Its appeal is foundational. Comforting. There is nothing wrong with having dirty thoughts.

C. Color. Soil color gives us an indication of how it behaves. Well drained soil tends to be light and bright. Wet soil tends to be dark. The mineral structure of the soil can be surmised by the color.

A. Aroma. You can develop a sense of the health of the soil by its aroma. It's easy to identify a soil that is depleted of nutrients or is toxically lacking oxygen by applying some good old fashioned olfaction sense.

S. Structure. When I make pancakes the batter binds together. It is an arrangement of components. The ingredients and the ratio of each impacts its standing and how they bind together. The components together provide the gravitas to the surroundings.

T. Texture. Soil is a combination of sand, silt and clay particles, most soils are a combination of the three. That combination tells us a lot of how that soil will behave. Potting soils are often a "soilless" mix designed and manufactured to create an environment suitable to contained habitat. A mix of organic matter like coconut coir or fiber, peat moss, a wetting agent, perlite, vermiculite, and sometimes a slow-release fertilizer. Without sand, silt, or clay involved, the mix technically isn't soil. Soil "to go" in our "on demand" culture is satisfying nonetheless.

Are you grounded?

On my radio show when people ask me "how are you?" I always say "staying grounded." I mean it. The minute you act like you're something important or special compared to others is the moment you will make a fool of yourself. We *are* in this together. We are gardeners and cultivators of our time together here on earth. It's about *how* you go about your business. Soil is the business side of cultivation, propagation and sustainability. And when you're grounded, my friend, you are better equipped to serve, support and contribute to others.

Rick Vuyst

I ate my vegetable
A practice commendable
My taste you may question
The greens for ingestion
Some find simply indigestible

Chapter Seventeen
The Kale of the Wild

AS A KID CHURCH POT-LUCKS WERE great, because they always involved cake with thick, liberal amounts of frosting. Go for the corner piece and there's more frosting. The downside of the pot-lucks was you had to choke down your token portion of a seven-layer salad some lady named Mable brought before you could have cake. The seven-layer salad is an all-American dish combining layers of iceberg lettuce, onions, tomatoes, water chestnuts, cucumbers, sweet peas, hard-boiled eggs, sharp cheddar cheese, and bacon. The colorful salad is topped off and frosted with a mayonnaise-based dressing and sometimes sour cream is added. It was presented in a glass pan or bowl so the layers could be admired before consumption. There of course were some redemptive qualities to the seven-layer salad namely three of them. One was the peas. The salad is known to have originated from the southern region of the United States and called "seven-layer pea salad" with multiple layers of peas. The naturally sweet legume is rich in essential vitamins, antioxidants and fiber. The second benefit was obviously bacon, because who doesn't like bacon? The third and final benefit was the fact that taking a chunk of the salad would take up space on my plate. It would free me from the guilt of avoiding a slab of Esther's jello salad, a gelatinous mess of marshmallows, fruit, glowing neon gelatin and who knows what else. Sorry, no more room on the plate. I'll come back later for seconds. Later never happened.

Nothing says "gathering" like the seven-layer salad. Nothing says ***family gathering*** like a seven-layer salad. You eat it off a paper plate with people you see once a year on the holidays. A staple of church pot-lucks or family holiday gatherings, don't leave it out in the sun too long, because you're taking some of it home with you as "leftovers" to remind you why you don't like seven-layer salad the rest of the week. You'll also inherit a Cool Whip™ container of the jello "salad" no one ate more appropriately referred to as jello mold which will promptly find its way to the trash can once you get home. The seven-layer salad I was accustomed to eating had a water chestnuts surprise in one of the layers. If you claim to like water chestnuts, you're lying. They were in the mix and laziness came into play as it is simply too much work to take the time to pick out the water chestnuts. Colorless filler, they sneak up on you and it's not polite to spit them out. It's like biting into a raw potato, the water chestnuts mask some of the guilt of eating a "salad" that is coated with bacon, sugar, sour cream and mayonnaise. A water chestnut will never taste good, so it has to be good for you right?

The word pot-luck first appeared as a word in the 16th century meaning, food provided for an unexpected or uninvited guest or the "luck of the pot." Some believe the "communal meal" where food was brought to pass with others, most likely originated in the 1930s during the Great Depression. I'll "pass" on the jello mold. Gatherings were far and few between in 2020 and I actually found myself missing the seven-layer salad as an occasional part of my diet.

When in doubt say, "I didn't have time to make a decorous meal" then add calorie-laden bleu cheese dressing, bacon bits and tomatoes on a quarter chunk of iceberg head lettuce and call it a wedge salad. A creamy bacon iceberg. Dead ahead! People spend big money plus a tip at a fancy steakhouse for one of these. Iceberg lettuce is appropriately named because it tastes like solidified water. At a time when we need unity more than ever, iceberg lettuce is trying to divide us and drive a wedge between us. There are those who say "why bother with the watery greens when arugula or kale are much more intriguing with their spiciness and earthiness?" The iceberg wedge is always served on a plate too small, and sawing through it with a steak knife results in half of it on the floor ... or your pants. Sooner or later you have to get up to use the restroom with dollops of bleu cheese dressing on your pants. Stay calm? If you can stay calm while all around you is chaos, then you probably haven't completely understood the situation. Maybe the iceberg wedge happened because a chef was too lazy or busy to chop, wash, and spin the lettuce before serving. The watery vegetation is blanketed in some of the fattiest ingredients around. When in doubt, put calorie-laden bacon, cheese and creamy sauces on food to make it exciting, A chunk of lettuce that is all dressed up with one place to go. Your stomach. They're guilt-free calories because, of course, we are eating salad.

I'm just an "Arugula" guy

Something tells me you're not just "arugula" person, you're special, so eat like it. With arugula maybe it's the fancy name also known as "roquette" that makes it sound more elitist and expensive than kale. You're "kaling" me here. Think about it. If you're comfortable with a scrambled egg and bacon sandwich for breakfast, a drive thru burger for lunch and a gourmet microwave frozen dinner after a long day, kale is a stretch. The general populace has an uneasy relationship with the leafy green and a reputation so revered it's considered a superfood akin to longevity vitamins. Kale has been designated the title "super food" though it's tough to chew and tends to be most popular after Christmas is over, right around the time of January New Year's resolutions and gym memberships. I like kale as a decorative plant but will opt for other greens first. In the era of "clean eating," internet wellness fads, and social media guilting, kale comes highly recommended by the internet wellness gurus. The allure is what I call the "kale of the wild." For some it's a tough chew with a mineral taste and a side of bitter. But don't admit it. You might not like the taste but you'll like how it makes you feel. You're a rebel, you're doing something. It's raw, it's natural, it's the wind through your hair. You've answered the call. You've responded to the kale of the wild!

It makes me sad that arugula trails kale and spinach in popularity. Arugula is great tasting, versatile and healthy but tagged with the moniker of a fancy, peppery, pungent, mildly bitter acrid flavored leafy green. Arugula originates in the coastal Mediterranean. Rocket or arugula is more commonly known outside the United States especially in Europe most notably Italy. The pungent edible leaves have been consumed for centuries and is mentioned in the Bible Old Testament Book of Kings. It was popular in Europe during the middle ages. A perfect partner to tomatoes and mozzarella cheese you can adorn the top of your pizza with its spicy goodness. Anything nicknamed "The Rocket" has got to be a blast to incorporate in your recipes. Arugula should be such an easy sell; it's certainly a hardy green and easier to grow than romaine. At the risk of a side salad of roquette making me appear aloof and hoity toity, it's fun to pronounce and adds some class to my day.

It's like mirepoix. A fancy name for chopped vegetables. Mirepoix is the fundamental element of classical cuisine. The workhorse, the flavor, the aroma in soups and dishes. Attempting to avoid an appendage accident, I love chopping up mirepoix and saying the word because it makes me look like I'm a chef and sound like I know what I'm doing. Essentially carrots, celery, and onions, when combined, these aromatics add flavor and aroma. When it comes to the fundamental element of ratios in Mirepoix I like to cut myself a break (poor choice of words) and feel free to eyeball it. I love celery but variations on a mirepoix theme that include bell peppers or leeks are something I like "shallot." I don't care, it's an opportunity to get creative with vegetables. If you're in culinary school trying to get a grade or a stickler for the rules you have to get the ratios right. At my age I'm up for a reasonable vegetable adventure and close enough is close enough. And just because it is alible doesn't mean I want to add it to the mix. Kohlrabi, which as a teen I thought was a foreign country, tastes like a combination of radishes and cabbage to me. I love radishes with a sprinkle of salt. Easy to handle and a bite-size treat of goodness. Kohlrabi, though interesting, trendy and decorative, is a stretch for me. In German, kohl means cabbage, and rabi means turnip, which is literally a good description. Kohlrabi tastes like cabbage and radishes, looks like a turnip, sounds like a foreign country and though alible is not going to be on my top-ten list for vegetables.

During the social distancing days of 2020 and lack of social gatherings, the pot-luck took a back seat and healthy eating in moderation became an emphasis. It takes a crisis to remind us that healthy eating, exercise, hydration and deep breathing are important disciplines for our physical and mental health. Growing your own vegetables is not that hard if you have sunshine, some good soil and a water source. View it as a "crop"-ortunity. An organic, nutrient-rich soil is a worthwhile investment, because remember when growing your own, you are what you eat. The activity of gardening alone is going to provide you fresh air and exercise. And when it comes to hydration of all foods, vegetables and fruits provide significant water with some being well over 80%

water by weight. Celery, bok choy, lettuce, cucumbers, tomatoes, zucchini and bell peppers, as examples, will whet your appetite. Fruits like watermelon, strawberries, cantaloupe and peaches provide such hydrating juicy goodness you'll wet your plants.

After years of helping people grow their gardens, I'm convinced, aside from sunshine and a good foundation of organic media to grow in, water is key to good cell-wall development in vegetables. Don't cycle between wet and dry. For the family Cucurbitaceae or cucurbits, also known as "vining vegetables," a good source of water at the base with good drainage is the key to keep disease like powdery or downy mildew at bay and develop sizeable fruit that is not bitter. Avoid water on the foliage of cucurbits in humid weather. If leaves stay wet all night in the humid air, problems like powdery mildew or downy mildew quickly get a foothold and will spread like wildfire with devastating results. You need to wet your plants, but do it right.

During a pandemic stay-home lockdown, many asked the question, can I grow an edible quarantine garden indoors? Adding supplemental light will be the key. There is a difference between what will grow and what will be successful. A plant like basil as an example needs a lot of sunlight and warm temperatures to grow properly. And an indeterminate tomato or vining squash isn't going to work. You're probably best sticking with some greens indoors. Easy to grow, high yield and low maintenance if you can add some supplemental light and water you can harvest indoors for some salads.

The topic came up on my radio show that deer pressure is a real problem for many who find themselves suddenly growing a plot of vegetables outdoors. Some of the deterrent methods were, well, should we say questionable. The spirit is willing but the fence is weak. You may have ray, a drop of golden sun, but doe, a deer, a female deer wants to eat the fruits of your labors. A barrier to thwart rabbits is much easier to establish than one that will de-ter a deer. The barrier would have to be substantial, resulting in a sizable investment and effort. An 8-foot-tall barrier is not practical or acceptable in many neighborhoods, and deer repellents can become expensive and annoying to continually apply. If you do apply just make sure the breeze is not blowing in your direction or you will smell like garlic and putrescent egg solids all day. Putrescent is a nice and important sounding way of saying rotting and decay. You can fire noise cannons intermittently or play recorded sound effects, but in most suburban neighborhoods that can easily get you kicked out of the association.

Idiosyncratic behavior

I have a friend who discovered the joys of gardening in 2020. A builder by trade now all he wants to do is garden. Understandable, he is reaching retirement age like me and that's what you do in retirement right? You garden. Ron is an idiosyncratic person who does it his way. *Idio* is ancient Greek for one's own or personal. An idiosyncratic person is someone who does things their own way like Frank Sinatra. Albert Einstein was like that too. Part of his genius was that he made sure to get 10 hours of sleep each day. There is a real mental benefit in getting enough sleep each night. Sleep is like vegetables, we all need more of it.

> *"It is a common experience that a problem difficult at night is resolved in the morning after the committee of sleep has worked on it."*
>
> *– John Steinbeck*

Einstein liked to walk. Exercise is healthy for our mental acuity, and theories abound that walking can boost memory, creativity and problem solving. Another notable idiosyncratic behavior of Einstein was he didn't wear socks. One of his eccentricities was an aversion to socks. They get holes in them so why bother.

I Need to Change My Plants

My friend Ron will show up in shorts and wide-open unlaced work boots, a T-shirt, sunglasses, unlit cigarette in his mouth, grey hair with a ponytail and a colorful bandana. Most people when initially finding an interest in gardening begin growing tomatoes, peppers, some lettuce and basil. Not him. He is an original. Pigweed became his edible plant of choice.

Pigweed or amaranth can be found almost everywhere from central Canada to Argentina The common name pigweed comes from its use as fodder for pigs. Effective at spreading its dust of seeds you will find it everywhere. Red amaranth's seed was a staple grain of the Aztec diet for making flour. Pigweed has been flourishing and feeding humans internationally for centuries. Pigweed plants are commonly considered to be weeds by farmers and gardeners, because they thrive in disturbed soils. Agricultural fields with exposed soils provided them their ideal habitat. The leaf arrangement resembles that of a poinsettia and in the case of redroot pigweed leaves with a purplish underside and a red tap root that is as colorful as Christmas.

Chenopodium album is another pigweed in the family Amaranthaceae which also goes by the names bacon weed, fat hen, goosefoot, lambsquarters or white goosefoot. Pick the tops from the summer-tall plants and prepare them as you would any green for a crunchy salad or sautéed as a side for your dinner or in an omelette. Many feel lambsquarters taste like spinach. Ron likes the fact they grow tall not prostrate so the tender new growth harvest is easily reachable and doesn't take a lot of room. In Jamaica, pigweed is known as callaloo and is a culinary staple. Beauty is in the eye of the beholder as its designation as a weed lies in the fact that each plant can produce upwards of 100,000 seeds, ensuring many generations per season. That makes it a menace for farmers as it competes with other crops they are trying to grow. They will grow faster than green grass goes through a goose as pigweed performs a type of photosynthesis called C4 carbon fixation. C4 plants are able to more efficiently absorb atmospheric carbon dioxide than C3 plants and are adapted to higher temperatures and drier conditions. You can accept compliments on their robust growth but the biggest benefit is this: the leaves of pigweed are very nutritious. They're high in vitamins A and C and folate, as well as calcium. The farmer might not agree with your idiosyncratic gardening habits but *bon appetit* Ron and to your health. Foraging "weeds" is not eccentric behavior. It's getting back to your roots.

Melissopalynology is not someone you dated in high school

Humans have five basic taste abilities, sweet, sour, bitter, salty, and umami, which is defined as savory. Umami, or the "fifth taste," is an aromatic and piquant flavor. We all know savory when we taste it, hard to put into words, so umami will have to do. Most of us however have a weakness and that is sweet things. In ancient times this discovery led people to rob the bee hives for sweeteners in foods and wine. Thus the practice of melissopalynology developed, which is the study of pollen in honey. The term comes from the Greek words for "bee" and "honey" and the "study of dust," or pollen. It is recognized worldwide as being the way to determine the floral contents and the geographical origin of honey. The palynologist in pollen analysis has plenty of sources to research. According to botanical records worldwide, there are over 350,000 angiosperms (flowering plants) from which honey bees can collect pollen and nectar. Variety is both the spice and sweetness of life in the natural world. The analysis of the honey works because (I'm told by my beekeeper friends) that honey bees have "floral fidelity." Each trip out of the hive they stick to one type of blossom.

With a weakness for sweets and a lifestyle that demands speed and convenience, an international crisis engaged a reset mechanism for survival among humans. Back to our roots. Eat more plants and the fruits of their labors as in vegetables and fruits. Get more fresh air. Move. The benefits of surviving the crux of exigency demands change and the long-term betterment of individuals who will be better equipped to help others in future endeavors or dilemmas. Together we help our kindred human beings.

Don't waste a crisis

We learned during a pandemic crisis that we as a society in general needed to make changes: to eat healthier and exercise more with plenty of fresh air. During a personal "crisis" years ago, I came to that realization and that was when I made running a personal habit. It changed my life. The change in behavior takes some effort, but it's all relative when put in perspective. You do your best to stay motivated and focused while you adapt to a healthy lifestyle. How do you do that? I've read that it takes 66 days to make a new habit, on average. Not sure how they figured that out but that's 1,584 hours of applied discipline. Once you get through it you have a healthy habit for life. If an average lifespan were 75 years, 1,584 hours is less than ¼ of one percent of your time invested in personal improvement. Seems like a good investment to me. Answer the call. The kale of the wild. And pass me some of that salad please?

Rick Vuyst

It's time to take a chance
A cause we can advance
Digging, cultivating, hoeing
We're going to get growing
I need to change my plants

Chapter Eighteen
I Need to Change My Plants

RABBITS AND DOGS CAN SMEUSE with the best of them. No, not schmooze as in the friendly persuasive manner we converse to gain favor, although I've seen some dogs adept at soliciting their owners for a treat. Rather, they smeuse, as in knowing the best cut throughs and escapes at the base of a hedge. A smeuse is a hole in the base of a hedge, made by small animals and habitually used. It's cartoonish in nature as the rabbit flees for cover closely chased by a dog through the same smeuse. The rabbit breaks for freedom on "smeuse control" and the dog is just being a dog.

When driving our cars in cruise control we are annoyed when having to detour or do a U turn. I did that just the other day when late for a meeting and added 20 minutes to my trip. I was late. It caused me to think what percentage of our day is spent on autopilot? Communicating, working, walking, eating, traveling; how much of the day is driven by habit? We are told we are creatures of habit, so is fifty percent of our day on autopilot? We know habits are hard to change. They're hard to change because they're ingrained, because they're almost automatic. And which of my behaviors are grounded in a well-rooted routine? Can I just slide by socially with my savoir faire competence honed by years of practice?

Being well grounded is an admirable characteristic to have. Like anything else however you can overdo a good thing. If you're too grounded you end up in a rut. And if your feet are always firmly on the ground, you'll have trouble putting on your pants.

> "If you want to make enemies, try to change something."
> – Woodrow Wilson

I have learned over time that there are three types of people in this world. Those who make things happen; those who watch things happen and those who wonder what in the world just happened. That never changes. But as I've aged I have learned an addendum is in order when it comes to competency in a given activity. It could be said that the three types of people are:

1. Those who learn by reading about it.
2. Those who learn by observation.
3. Those who have to screw up first to learn their lesson.

How many times have people approached me and said, "I have a brown thumb." Whatever the job, whatever the activity including plant care, most people with the right attitude are teachable. And if you haven't killed any plants you're not trying hard enough. The key that unleashes the potential is purpose. Purpose is the fuel that sees any activity through from germination to growth to success. Gardening is no different. Healthy lifestyle, growing your own food, beauty, property value, exercise, rehabilitation; there are a plethora of purposeful reasons to engage with plants. Purpose provides clarity which is just like pruning. Remove what isn't needed and shed light on what is good.

Everyday brings its crop of successes and failures. And when you fail it is important to *remember that failure is simply success in progress.* The lesson learned is you have to get up the next day and face the words and the deeds of the previous day. I remind myself of this everyday I go to work; it is an excellent mental rudder to have in the water as you navigate daily, choppy seas. Own your mistakes and ask the question, how is it one careless match can start a forest fire, but it takes a whole box to start a campfire?

Bramblings

Voltaire, the French enlightenment writer and philosopher famous for his witty works of satire in *Candide*, intended for us, when all is said and done, to simply tend to our own garden first. I recognize I need to do that so I am better equipped to deal with the changes. As I was taught as a child in my ecclesiastical studies, "What has been will be again, what has been done will be done again; there is nothing new under the sun." Maybe that is why something as old as dirt rejuvenates us and awakens our senses with each new and changing season. Dirt, foliage and the desire to cultivate is not new under the sun, but it rejuvenates dependably, and that is a comforting thought as we tend to our garden.

So life is a bramble like the biennial canes of raspberries or blackberries. Seasons come and go. The presence of both thorns and edible fruit. In the rose family we learn to take the good with the bad. Sometimes in a tangle, a good pruning is needed. A reset.

> ***"Life is bristling with thorns, and I know no other remedy than to cultivate one's garden."***
>
> *– Voltaire*

"That's all very well put," says Candide in Voltaire's novel, "but we must go and work our garden." Candide's kick in our plants was metaphorical not literal. However Voltaire himself really believed that active gardening was a great way to stay healthy and manage stress. A purpose. We now know from science he was ahead of his time. Aside from the obvious fresh air, exercise and movement, we know there is a lessening of depression in patients in recovery. Structured gardening activities give patients an existential purpose. And purpose helps give daily life meaning. There is no doubt purpose can often be found in your pain because the experience sticks with you. Think of the plant chamomile, which is most useful when trampled on or crushed ... it just makes "scents."

> *"Our critics are our friends. They show us our faults."*
>
> *– Ben Franklin*

The (garden) plot:

We as humans like patterns so we can anticipate what's going to happen. That's why we love the seasons. We celebrate them with almost a Pavlovian response. A seasonal cadence. There is a rhythm to life. Seasons. When facing change the question that should be asked is "what's the worst that could happen?" It changes the thought process and dynamics of processing when dealing with an issue. Lack of knowledge is the number one impediment to change. "I have no idea what awaits me over there." Like my friend Stephen always says "You don't know what you don't know." He is the same person who always reminds me that "things aren't as good as they seem and things aren't as bad as they seem." I like to play the "on a scale of 1 to 10" game with people. It's a quick litmus test to gauge the variation in opinion on what's anticipated. You need to allow space for inevitable change or seasons as part of the overall plan. And if you're always tuned in to WIIFM (what's in it for me?) you're often going to be unhappy. Take your lesson from plants; they give more than they take.

> *If we are truly resistant to change then why does the grass seem greener on the other side of the fence? Because it has to be our idea. Change is difficult. Forced change is much harder.*

I suppose it's human nature to want to over prepare when there is anxiety for a coming change or threat. And when a few people do it, it doesn't take long for others to follow suit – a domino effect because no one wants to feel left out. Don't label me an old mumpsimus. When dealing with the anticipatory anxiety they feel good about the fact they did something about it. It restored some sense of having control. Fear happens to people who are big into anticipation. It can be difficult to keep your mind where your body is and deal with it when the time comes. It's good to have a vision; it's smart to plan ahead, but not *worry* ahead. A healthy serving of faith with a side of optimism will ground you.

> *"The only thing that is constant is change."*
> *–Turkish philosopher,*
> *Heraclitus (535-475 BC)*

As new ideas or solutions are germinated, embracing the "what if" approach makes things happen. I've always been oriented that way. If seeds are planted we feed them with "what if." It's the sunshine that makes ideas grow. Those who immediately come up with reasons why it won't work never cease to amaze or frustrate me. In a group setting you can see those who are busy formulating in their mind a list of why the concept won't work even as it's being presented. What follows is a litany of excuses and reasons why it's never going to work. There are always elements of a plan that won't work, but the mindset of "what if" unlocks the potential of what is good and fertilizes the concept.

> **I need to change my plants:** When your focus changes from giving me "reasons it won't work" to "giving a season to try" you never know what may happen until you do.

Don't be a Prickly Pear Cactus (easily offended) with an "It can't be done" attitude. When people are burned or poked by change they become that much more resistant to future change. They become wired to protect a position. "I have a brown thumb, everything I touch dies." That's a piece of information I would have liked before you shook my hand.

Change is not an excuse to give up. It's an opportunity to GROW.

One of the keys to positive change is don't be consumed by "what's going to happen?" Rather focus on what might be the end goal or result of that change. Mentally minimize the threat and maximize the reward. You have to have a sense of humor to deal with change because we are wired to resist. When people are burned by change, they become that much more resistant to future change. "I have a brown thumb." Get ahead of change instead of reacting to it. Seeking sublimity is not *enduring* life's vexations but rather a celebration of the journey along a foliaceous path that matters: making new friends, recognizing there are those set in your path to enrich, straighten and share.

Move forward. And it has always bothered me that we use the phrase "back and forth." How can we go back if we haven't gone forth yet? It's backwards. Better to go "to and fro" but if you say that people will look strangely at you. It seems to me more than ever before you are either moving forward or backwards but very little stays the same. The "same" can feel and smell like stagnant water in the bottom of a pot. You can live with it for a while but eventually the drainage hole has to be unplugged. If not, the default mode will be eventual decline. And growth sure beats going backwards. That's why people love plants. That's why in a crisis people turn to plants. **Growth is synonymous with moving forward.** It's why the adjective "blooming" is analogous to a person growing, glowing, vigorous, flourishing or prospering.

Sometimes when you don't have a solution, it's good to admire the problem.

Take as an example how we plant trees. We plant trees in *round* holes because it is the "norm." Pots are round. We plant the trees in a "foreign" soil in a round hole instead of facilitating a mix that involves or includes the existing native parent soil. Can't we just get along? Then we mound a volcano of mulch at the base because that's what our neighbors are doing; it's the "norm." Don't trust Norm. What do we think is going to happen? Just like the roots of that tree we go around in circles. A group mentality. Plant that tree in a square hole

> **I need to change my plants:** When you change your attitude from "I'll believe what I think" to "I'll test what I think" you are extending roots. There is a big difference between being planted and being buried.

next time. Blend the foreign amendments with the existing parent soil. Plant at a depth that provides a solid foundation but doesn't sink or "bury alive" the roots. A plant with unhealthy, unhappy roots will show its true colors above the surface every time. You can't hide it.

The Garden invites us to live in liminal space. We find liminal space by putting our hands in the dirt.

The word liminal comes from the Latin word *limen*, meaning threshold. Any point or place of entering or beginning. A liminal space is the time between the past and what is coming next. Not living in the past and not knowing what the future will bring as in: it's not settled yet. We hope for a harvest but it's not time yet. It's planting, it's cultivating without knowing what comes next. It's weird, yet a beautiful "in between space." It is a place of transition, a season of waiting, and not knowing. I have had to learn to live in that space. A place to plant seeds. We discover beauty sometimes in the most unexpected liminal places, because that's where God hides His greatest treasures. And what could be more marginalized than dirt? Yet it's the foundation of many beautiful things. The aroma of soil in spring when the winter is past is a liminal space. And whether it's people or plants, I always believe there is more good than is initially seen.

Many times it is found at the margins because there is purpose, beauty, great expectations to be found in the margins. The garden is a great place to celebrate margins. The margins have good circulation and exposure. Think of the garden in the book of Genesis. It's not land, it's not sky, it's the place in between, a garden. And we are called to cultivate and celebrate it with those around us ... weeds and all.

Your purpose is often embedded in the pain. It is only natural that spring follows winter.

Liminal space is where transformation takes place, if we are patient and let it shape us. And people enjoy a space that belongs to everyone. A natural space, a sacred space. A new appreciation for a space we took for granted. It's called being grounded. It's called a community garden. If we don't encounter liminal space in our lives, we start idealizing what we assume to be "normalcy," and trust me, no two seasons are the same. When "normal" doesn't happen it upends the status quo. There is a ripple effect. Like the changing soil temperature in spring, unseen to the eye, the ripple effect is an explosion of growth eventually evident to all. It is these transitions that are an invitation to growth. Nature shows us time and again. If you can find a way to live within a liminal space between the past and the future mentally, it is calming. So why does change often intimidate and cause so much stress? Because it tends to come at you fast. Change accelerates.

Change accelerates

Change is not only constant, it accelerates. It becomes difficult to keep up and the default response to the question "how are you?" shifts from "fine" or "good" to "busy." I think we love gardening because it is linear in a world where technological progress is exponential. Technology today progresses so fast that the linear expectations of preparation, plant, nurture and harvest has a comforting effect on our personal state. Progressively predictable. It's like the organized races I run in. I have never run in a race where they have moved the finish line once the race has started. Your progress along the course is progressively predictable and there is comfort in that. The major distinction between linear and exponential functions is the rate of their growth. That's what makes the garden such a great place. The growth is at a pace with seasonally embraced changes. It is true in a digital and computer age that we need more tactile experiences, and gardening provides that lifestyle ... a natural progressive experience.

American engineer and businessman, Gordon Moore, at one time was asked to predict technology change over a decade. Moore eventually settled on a time frame of "technology" (the number of transistors in a dense integrated circuit) doubling every few years. He later predicted a doubling every year in the number of components per integrated circuit and projected this rate of growth would continue for decades. The anticipation of technological change became known as Moore's Law. Regardless of how you look at it, the cost of computer technology to the consumer became affordable and convenient, and the world and how we live our daily lives changed rapidly. When it comes to technology, change accelerates. And what's the fastest path to irrelevance? Simple. Don't change.

With turmoil comes true innovation and change. Doors are opened to do things better and differently. **Change is an opportunity to grow.** For those who are young change affects their destiny. For those who are older change affects their legacy.

Consider this from the Tacoma News Tribune, April 11, 1953. Mark Sullivan the president of Pacific Telephone and Telegraph said in a speech, "Just what form the future telephone will take is of course pure speculation. Here is my prophecy. In its final development, the phone will be carried about by the individual perhaps as we carry a watch today. It probably will require no dial or equivalent and I think the users will be able to see each other, if they want, when they talk." Prophetic words of change. Long distance calls used to be expensive. Weekday minutes were especially expensive. Evening and weekend minutes were less expensive. Remember telling relatives you would call them after 6PM on the weekend? Now that's irrelevant. Payphones are gone. It has been said change is inevitable except from payphones and vending machines. Even that isn't true anymore. Culture and technology advances never seek permission to change. They just change. Past and present crises have caused significant change whether you're coming along or not.

Baby Bloomers

Consider the Baby Boomers who were not born with these technological advantages, but were forced to assimilate them into their daily lives and embrace advances as they aged or risk getting run over or left behind. I am one of those "Boomers" and affectionately refer to the group as Baby "Bloomers." As the "Bloomers" started families and purchased homes, the interest in lawn and gardening grew. Gardening was the weekend passion for many of this generation. Weekend warriors. But interest in plants continues to be strong as the "Bloomers" retire, evident by the Millenials and new generations and their passion to nurture growth. A new generation of plant lovers sprouts with each generation. And that's where something I call ***Rick's Law*** comes into play. Rick's Law is simple. The faster technology grows and impacts our lives and the crazier the world gets, there is an equal reaction and longing for plants, soil, flowers and the nurture of foliage. Back to the garden. Our roots. When technology takes the delay out of world-wide communication, it increases the longing for quiet time with earthy things. The goal isn't to mimic rapidly changing culture, because once you do, it will change again. The goal is to find comfort in getting grounded.

When I turned 60 a friend told me to look at it this way. That I had made it to third base. I think I would like to stand here a while. I'm tired but I'm not ready to go home yet.

Nature reminds us in so many ways that change is inevitable and in many cases good. Aside from the obvious weather and seasonal changes, like fall color, nature reminds us it is not in a static state, but rather a living, growing, ever-changing environment in both big and subtle ways.

Dance of the Detritivores

Consider the dance of the detritivores. The detritivores sound like a science fiction cast of characters sent to earth to wreak havoc until a superhero intervenes and saves the world. The reality is they are tiny organisms that feed on and break down dead plant or animal matter. Think composting; they are returning essential nutrients to the ecosystem. Detritivores include microorganisms such as bacteria and protists. Not the kind of "protisters" you would find at a political event. The most famous of the protists are simple multicellular organisms known as Amoeba, an animal-like protist that can be found in soil as well as in a freshwater and marine environment. They don't get a lot of attention, which is probably why some people mistakenly thought Amoeba was a tropical island you would visit for a winter getaway to use up some frequent-flyer miles.

Now before you "protist" that I forgot about the Myxomycetes, also called Mycetozoa, let me say they create change in a magical way. Slime molds are a phylum of fungus-like organisms within the kingdom Protista. The plot thickens right? They usually occur in decaying material like fallen logs or the bark mulch in your landscape right outside your window. The vegetative phase consists of a multinucleate amoeboid mass or sheet called plasmodium. The plasmodium with cytoplasm streaming through it, ***changes*** shape as it crawls over wood, leaves, bark mulch or soil, ingesting bacteria, molds, and fungi. Characteristically, the entire plasmodium is covered by a layer of slime, which is continually secreted and, as the plasmodium creeps, continually left behind as a network of collapsed tubules. Plasmodia are many times yellow or buff but can also be red, white and orange. On a warm, humid summer day, I can find it on hydrophobic areas of bark mulch, and it looks like a dog has vomited a bottle of mustard. I can poke and change it with a stick and it will reform. When this slime was created they broke the mold. Spores release one or more individual cells known as myxamoebae, which may transform into swarm cells with two flagella or whiplike structures used for "swimming." And wasn't the flagella one of the ships on which Columbus sailed the ocean blue? These guys know how to party. Everyone in the pool!

The detritivores dance in all ecosystems by getting rid of decaying organic matter left behind by other organisms. An agent of change, detritivores commonly play the role of decomposers. Change isn't always complicated. The detritivores, as change agent decomposers, teach us that the separation of constituent parts or elements into simpler compounds can be done without dramatics. The Myxomycetes however are more colorful and entertaining with a flair for the dramatic. You know them, the life of the party. While the detritivores dance quietly in the corner of the room the myxomycetes call attention to themselves. Like people who are the life of the party, they know how to make an entrance; they make their own fashion statement; they can celebrate at a moment's notice and can get along with almost anyone. Together the introverted detritivores and the extroverted myxomycetes are microscopic agents of change.

Jejune is not a good season.

When it comes to dramatic change, lightning knows how to conduct itself. Lightning is an explosive agent of change more dramatic than the methodical detritivores. Ever notice outdoors the morning after an overnight storm, how the landscape seems changed, renewed and green? I was struggling to figure out how lightning works, and then it struck me. Nitrogen in the atmosphere can be changed into a plant-usable form by supercharged lightning, a process called nitrogen fixation. Each bolt of lightning carries electrical energy that is powerful enough to change the nitrogen molecule in the atmosphere. Nitrogen bonds to oxygen in the atmosphere, forming nitric oxide. In essence a natural source of nitrogen oxides occurs from a lightning stroke. The nitric oxide reacts with more oxygen to form nitrogen dioxide. Along with the lightning during the storm come raindrops. Nitrogen dioxide dissolves in water which forms nitrates. The nitrates fall to the ground and dance on the foliage in raindrops in a form that can be absorbed by plants.

A final natural example is how we can step in and change things through crop rotation. Land itself can become "tired" and less fertile, because the same type of crop is planted repeatedly in the same area. The land is depleted of the nutrients needed for that plant's growth. Disease and pests can reach levels that are hard to control when they learn to hang out near a field that always has the same type of crop. Soil can also become susceptible to erosion if the same crop is used year after year. There is a great word to describe this boring unchanging condition. Jejune. Devoid of significance or interest, or, in a word ... dull. Lacking nutritive value. Best said by Aldous Huxley who envisioned a brave new world, "Habit converts luxurious enjoyments into dull and daily necessities." You have to shake things up. I need to change my plants.

The Understory

She called and left a message on my office phone. Not unusual, people message me all the time about a plant problem. This message however was different. As a broadcaster I both talk and listen to many people. You exercise your ability to both tell stories and listen to them. Everyone has a story but you can tell if there is something hiding inside. If you listen carefully the person inside will always find its way out. She had a plant that was "dying" and needed help.

I heard pain in her voice. She didn't volunteer her story but I heard it in her voice. Detecting emotion in text and emoji reliance can be difficult. But I believe as humans we are wired to pick up on emotions and have empathy with keen vocal recognition capabilities. I think when undistracted by visual cues we focus better. We can identify other's emotions through facial expressions, but our sense of hearing may be as strong as sight in detecting emotion. It's what I call the "understory."

Understory plants fill the void between the canopy of a forest and the ground floor. Vital to wildlife and the ecology of a woodland or rainforest environment, these plants thrive under the shade of more dominant and established trees. The plants are afforded protection or cover, and rely on "sunflecks" or "sunpatches" for photosynthesis. This irradiance to the forest floor is essential to survival. Plants subject to short periods of irradiation adapt rapidly, a "strike while the iron is hot" approach. Stomatal opening and closing (how a plant breathes) of plants adapted to understory conditions open faster during moments of sunshine than the stomata of intolerant and unadapted species. You could say the understory plants welcome and receive the benefit with grateful recipience. I love walks in the woods and an up-close interaction with the fledgling understory plants. As the foliage canopy flitters in the breeze, the available sunlight creates a theatrical dance of light and shadows below and adds to the magic of a woodland area.

I decided to make a house call at the home of the individual who had called me for advice. My schedule was full, but based on something I had heard in her voice, I fit the visit into my schedule. Maybe she had heard something in my voice on the radio that caused her to believe I could help her. She met me at the door and took me to the side yard to show me a struggling dogwood tree. The leaves were drooping and spotted with purple margins. She then proceeded to tell me the tree had not bloomed in spring the past two years. "The tree is dying" she said, and the tears started to flow. Instead of diagnosing the plant problem, I stopped, realizing she had a people "understory." I learned the tree had been gifted to her to memorialize the death of a loved one and she was losing hope. She had nurtured, watered, fertilized and prayed over the tree, all to no avail. I thought of how years ago in a more rural society a lilac would be planted when a child died and would grow and continue to bloom despite being neglected years later on old, abandoned farmhouse properties.

She apologized and I told her that I understood. Everyone has an understory. The tree was not dying but had to move. The location where it was planted was in a southwest exposure subject to heat and wind in summer and sun and winds in winter. The foliage problems were caused by a disease called anthracnose and could be addressed. The exposed location and reflection from the home's siding was stressing a plant native to understory conditions. Finally the exposed area for a tree already under stress was causing the swelling buds in spring to freeze before being able to bloom. The deck was stacked against this tree but all was not lost. There was hope.

That's when the words came out of my mouth, "You need to change your plants."

She said, "Excuse me?" and together we laughed.

I proposed we replace the tree in the current location with some hardy deciduous flowering shrubs and move the tree to the northeast side of the house. There the tree would still receive sunlight but would be given protection, both structural from the home and from the surrounding evergreen trees.

We did just that and I am happy to say the following spring the tree blossomed. She emailed me recently to say "the tree had blossomed for the second year in a row and looks happy and thank you, you knew that I needed to change my plants."

I've learned from the Oakley's in my life that when light is shined on an understory everyone benefits. We all learn. When the light shines on your understory it allows both you and others to breathe. We're in this together. You're not alone. Stories take us back to emotions and feelings we have in common. If you're struggling, hang in there, if anything you will inspire others.

We ***know*** bare soil is not a natural condition. *Something* is going to grow, fill the space and it will change. We ***know*** the seasons change. We ***know*** change is coming. Don't stick your head in the sand. Maybe Albert Einstein was right, "Any fool can know. The point is to understand." I need to change my plants.

A place of personal pardon
Where resentment doesn't harden
A refuge of my own
Over time it has grown
Grace exists in a verdant garden

Chapter Nineteen

Under the Vine and Fig

PAMELA LOOKED UP FROM HER phone and unsolicited out of the blue asked me, "If you could go back to the past or go to the future which would you choose?" I asked her if I chose the past could I know what I know today or would that be erased if I went back? If I know what I know now I would be dangerous. My friend and mentor Skip tells me I tend to move back and forth between past and present tense. I feel the tension. During an international pandemic in 2020 many in the process of looking back at what had happened and looking to an uncertain future experienced listlessness and depression. Isolation and loneliness affect mental health, and if there ever was a time to love your neighbor as yourself this was it. Paying attention to those around you and their mental health, as well as physical health, to mitigate those feelings of worry, stress, fear, anxiety and loneliness. If we were all in this together as we were told, we needed to encourage our neighbor that there was always hope. An epidemic of depression was all around us. We needed to be attentive to our brothers and sisters in this fight because "if only" is a painful phrase. If only we knew what was going on. If only they knew they weren't alone. If only we had recognized the signs.

After an exhausting and stressful day I sat alone, closed my eyes, and repeated the compelling image from Micah that everyone shall sit under his vine and under his fig tree, and no one shall make them afraid. A favorite passage of mine I imagine sitting in the shade of the vine and fig. When this is over I thought, *I will strive to encourage both myself and others to find their vine and fig and rest in its shade.* The phrase was used repeatedly in history during periods of stress and most notably by America's founders in correspondence when dealing with the strain of tyranny and the fight for independence.

The Cinchona tree to the rescue

Soon after the opening salvos of the American revolution George Washington was on a mission. As the colonists battled the gloomy sophisms of tyranny and anarchy as phrased by Alexander Hamilton in the Federalist papers, Washington knew he had a secret weapon against the British. He convinced the Continental Congress to spend $300 for quinine to protect the troops.

Quinine is isolated from the bark of the Cinchona tree and is native to Peru and South America. Bark extracts had been used to treat malaria since the 1600s and were introduced to Spain by Jesuit missionaries from the New World. The people of Peru, Colombia, Ecuador, and Venezuela had already been using quinine for generations when in the 17th century it was used to treat the Spanish Countess of Chinchon for malaria. Botanist Carl Linnaeus called the tree "Cinchona" in her honor.

Washington urged Congress to buy up as much cinchona bark and quinine powder as possible. General Washington was already personally using quinine when he petitioned Congress as he suffered from recurrent bouts of malaria since first contracting the disease in his teen years. The British were drastically short of Peruvian Spanish supplied quinine in this fight. And by 1779 Spain had declared war on Great Britain, creating a de facto alliance with the Americans compounding the British problems and supply.

The first years of the revolutionary war George Washington had used his troops in a cat-and-mouse-game overmatched and tailoring exposure to fight for another day. Disease opened the door to opportunity when General Cornwallis took the battle to the south and the mosquito and malaria helped turn the tide for independence. The British had walked into a mosquito maelstrom. The mosquito was merciless with unrelenting attacks on British troops lacking quinine during the British southern campaign and the capture of Charleston, a strategic port city. The Redcoats ensuing problems were less the Continental Army and more so the annoying buzzing disease-carrying insect called the mosquito. The area was a mosquito haven and the insect would pester the British relentlessly. The Brits swatting forces were much more susceptible to malaria than the American's better quinine-equipped and acclimated colonial troops. Once again plants had saved the day as in the cinchona tree and quinine extract.

An Ounce of Prevention

The founding fathers knew an ounce of prevention could lead to a cure for what ailed them. One of America's founding fathers, Ben Franklin, famously wrote: "An ounce of prevention is worth a pound of cure." Franklin, who made determinations based on evaluation of data or observation, would have arguably been the best founding father to analyze procedural efforts in a pandemic. He is the one who espoused the theory that illness was "spread by contagion," and made people sick with the common cold and flu. The conventional wisdom of the day was the common cold was caused by dampness in the air or from wearing wet clothing. In 1773, Benjamin wrote his friend Dr. Benjamin Rush, a signer of the United States Declaration of Independence and a civic leader in Philadelphia, his theory that people "often catch cold from one another when shut up together in close rooms, coaches, etc., and when sitting near and conversing so as to breathe in each other's transpiration." He felt contagion from the common cold was caused by passing droplets from person to person and not just damp, cold or wet air which exacerbated the situation.

Years later on December 12, 1799, on a miserable day of rain, snow and sleet, George Washington rode horseback on his appointed rounds surrounding Mount Vernon. He was late returning that evening so his dinner guests had already arrived. Washington chose not to change out of his wet clothes so he wouldn't keep them waiting. Each day Washington would mount his horse and ride around his property for hours, checking on projects. He would then return from a long day of riding at dinner time. There were always visitors for dinner. That had to be wearisome. Some visitors were family members, but many complete strangers who would show up with a letter of introduction from a mutual friend. It's amazing to think that after leaving office on March 4, 1797, Washington had an open-door policy at Mount Vernon receiving guests who wanted to mingle with the former president.

Again the next day, despite wintery conditions and feeling ill, Washington braved the elements to assess improvements to Mount Vernon. He probably thought nothing of it, after all he had survived the winter of 1777-1778 with his troops at Valley Forge and its hardships. With chest congestion, sore throat and difficulty breathing, on the evening of December 14, 1799, at Mount Vernon, George Washington passed away of a throat infection. He was buried four days later in the family vault at

Mount Vernon. If today's modern medical procedures had been available to him he most likely would have survived. Using methods of the day they had him drink a concoction of molasses butter and vinegar and he was bled. Bloodletting was a medical treatment common at the time that did more harm than good. They believed all of these remedies would draw the "bad humours" out of his blood, but nothing worked. The "Founding Father" of America was dead.

Long prior to his death, Washington would imagine his appointed time under the vine and fig. The Treaty of Paris in 1783 had formally ended the American Revolutionary War. With the war now behind him Washington wrote to the Marquis de Lafayette in 1784, "At length my dear Marquis I have become a private citizen on the banks of the Potomac and under the shadow of my own vine & my own fig tree." Soon however he would be tapped to be our first president called again to public service serving from 1789 to 1797. But he never lost sight of his desire to sit safely under his own vine and fig tree.

> *"Everyone will sit under their own vine and under their own fig tree, and no one will make them afraid, for the Lord Almighty has spoken."*
>
> *– Micah 4:4 (NIV)*

Washington often used this biblical reference in his writings. He would reference Micah as a means to express a desire for a state of bliss free of the ardor of war and contest with Britain. Upon leaving the presidency he wanted to leave public life stating, "I am now seated in the shade of my own vine and fig tree, and shall devote the remainder of a life, nearly worn out to such agricultural and rural amusements as will afford employment for myself, and cannot, or ought not, to give offense to anyone; offering while I am on this theatre, my sincere vows that the ravages of war, and the turbulence of passions; may yield their scepters to peace and tranquility."

Ficus carica or fig trees have an interesting peculiarity that the blossoms of the fruit appear before the leaves. Naturally we look for fruit on a tree in full leaf. But not with a fig tree. In temperate climates like the Mediterranean, the early fruit, or blossoms, appear in spring before the leaves open, on branches of the last year's growth, and the first ripe fruit is ready in June or earlier. The late figs grow on the new wood and keep appearing during the later season. Fig, (*Ficus carica*) is a plant in the mulberry family Moraceae. Most trees or plants in that family produce fleshy fruits with seeds including a favorite of mine Jackfruit, *Artocarpus heterophyllus*. Jackfruit is great mixed with barbecue sauce on a bun, and if you close your eyes it tastes like pulled pork without the meat.

You may have to settle with dwelling under a mulberry tree as here in the midwest or northeast US it's tough to dwell under the shade of the fig. Figs are best grown in USDA Zones 8-10 in organically rich, moist, well-drained soils in full sun to part shade. You can have some hit or miss luck in USDA Zones 6 and 7 with a south-facing wall and a good layer of mulch, but plants will experience significant die-back in cold winters. And if grown in containers, you're going to have to bring them in for winter. Fig cultivars like 'Brown Turkey' and 'Chicago Hardy' do have some good relative winter hardiness.

The Viners, Twiners and Whiners ... a matter of perseverance

Aside from the figs, now vines, that's a whole other matter. A vine can be relentless. Take the wisteria vine as an example. It can look old tired and gnarly but looks can be deceiving. In short order it can swallow a trellis or pergola. A woody vine, the scandent tendrils of wisteria can consume an entire fence, arbor, and in lore and legend has done so to small houses. A true "viner" they will grow and grow in lieu of blooming unless you show it who is boss with a little bit of stress and root pruning.

The moonflower and morning glory vines are ethereal twiners but don't let that fool you. Ipomoea alba, or moonflower, is part of the family Convolvulaceae which includes morning glory and the less welcome bindweed, one of the more difficult to eradicate weeds of the temperate garden. The Ipomoea genus can reach out, pirouetting in their predetermined, typically clockwise direction, seeking something to entwine with its tendrils. One of the things that stops their twining dead in their tracks is frost. You can't even say that word around them. It is notorious for quickly making us the gardener "whiners" when the vines ignore us to incessantly grow without producing blooms. It's at that point we have to reestablish its priorities with some stress to get it to bloom.

I'm sure the vine Micah had in mind, as well as Washington, were grape vines. But what I like about vines in general however is they do not let obstacles get in the way. I wish I could get some people to take on a vine mentality. You've seen them I'm sure. When a new concept is proposed or new ideas, you can see some people in the room quickly formulating reasons "why this will never work" in their mind even before the conclusion of the presentation. When given the chance to speak they have already formulated a list of excuses, reasons and arguments why the idea will never work. They throw up a wall. This drives me crazy. "Di-Vine" intervention is sometimes needed. Debate is fine but blockage for the sake of blockage drives me nuts. What I like about vines is they

> **I need to change my plants:** When you change your attitude from "burdened" to "pruned" you open up your vista to enlightenment.

ignore the naysayers. They go up, around, under, through, horizontal, vertical, sideways and don't let an obstacle like a fence, wall, space or humans get in their way or discourage them. I was sent a picture from a person who had a landscape vine grow through the siding on the outside of the house and find its way into a heat duct and eventually through the register into the living room. We call that persistence.

I tend not to have a lot of patience with "whiners" who have a victim mentality day in and day out and wallow in negativity forcing it upon others like weeds. The attitude is like bindweed with querulous tendrils covert in nature, before you know it they have wrapped you in their reach. I'm suspicious when "everyone else" causes their misery and "nothing they do will ever make a difference." Wallowing in misery isn't necessarily unhealthy for a short period of time. It helps with acknowledging and processing painful emotions but you have to move on. I usually decide to give them a nudge followed by a kind but supportive kick in the plants, especially when their verbalized attitude comes in three waves: Wave 1, "Bad things always happen to me." Wave 2, "Those people or those circumstances are to blame." Wave 3, "Nothing's going to change; there's no point in trying." Time for some pruning.

I spend a large share of the day talking to myself and I know you do too. How you talk to yourself can lead to self sabotage. In real life at some point you're going to be "pruned." You can mope or you can bloom. You can shade everyone's party or be the life of the party.

Weeds will do what weeds will do. And nature will be nature which is not always calm and "normal." We have to adapt. Celebrate and live with nature. The more we poke the bear, nature will be nature. We shouldn't be surprised things happen. We're in this together, you, me and nature.

Even though we are called to live in the present liminal space, we can look to the past for understanding and to the future with hope, because where there is no vision there is division. Don't wait for someone else to do it for you. There are countless ways you can plant seeds today in your own personal story.

Plant some seeds

Don't be a whiner. Growth comes when you are willing to invest in yourself. Not short-term investments but longer-term, investments that pay off in 5, 10, 20 years. And revel in the fact that some seeds you plant may not fruit for you but will benefit others down the road. A legacy. I believe you're planting when you make investments in these fruits available to you starting today.

- **Reading**. It puts your brain to work, expands your horizons and is a form of personal meditation that unplugs you from the bustle and noise of life all around you.
- **Writing**. Pick up a pen. Write it down. Developing your writing skills helps you sort your thoughts and plan. You can go back to it to review. It will improve your memory.
- **Faith**. It provides purpose in life, a deep-rooted, meaningful belief of good things to come.
- **Exercise**. Invest in your body, brain and mental health.
- **Invest income.** No matter how little, I found far more long-term satisfaction from saving as opposed to spending.
- **Invest in others**. Helping others provides purpose in life.
- **Seek out "Oakleys"** on your path in your life. They will teach you a lot. You can't possibly live long enough to make all the mistakes yourself so learn from others. I call it investing your "learnings."

- **Dream**. If we truly spend 25% of our day talking to ourselves make it positive. It will reinforce your behavior.

The best time to plant a tree was 20 years ago. The next best time is today. At some point you will be seeking out the shade of your vine and fig. Give it some time to grow.

Plants impact history

Plants have impacted the course of history in many ways. Think of the impact of rice, coffee, cotton, bamboo, rubber for tires, wheat, sugarcane, tobacco, wine grapes and corn just to name a few. Plants impacted the course of history in medicine, building materials, food and fuel. From shelter to shade to sustenance, they will always be foundational to progress and life. Think about the coconut. It's a stretch to think the professor could make a radio out of a coconut on Gilligan's island, but the simple coconut and tree can be used for food and milk, water and oil, husks for scrubbing, to crafts and ropes to thatched roofs for shelter, brooms and fuel for fires, coir for soil medias to mats and so much more. Plants have always been there (technically from day three) the foundational genesis of why in crisis we go back to our roots.

Look at how the potato alone impacted the US with the significance of the Irish Potato Famine. The Irish Potato Famine, also known as the Great Hunger, began in 1845 when the potato pathogen *Phytophthora infestans*, the causal agent of potato late blight, impacted humanity and drove a flood of immigrants to America, changing the face of our country. The pathogen spread rapidly throughout Ireland, and because the farmers of Ireland relied heavily on the potato as a source of food, the infestation had a catastrophic impact on Ireland and its population. It is estimated roughly one million Irish died from starvation and related causes, with at least another million forced to leave their homeland as refugees. Irish immigration to the United States during the Great Famine had a lasting impact on the economy and culture of the United States. Millions of Americans can claim Irish ethnicity traced back to their ancestry and the potato famine years. Irish immigrants poured into New York City, and significantly contributed to the labor force, impacted the culture and soon after immigrating, found themselves fighting in the Civil War. Most had found their way here due to the simple *Solanum tuberosum,* or potato, and the collapse of it as a food source due to a pathogen. The rest is history.

> *"Everyone can recognize history when it happens. Everyone can recognize history after it has happened; but it is only the wise person who knows at the moment what is vital and permanent, what is lasting and memorable."*
> – *Winston Churchill*

Plants helped save the day

My personal mental maelstrom is that I swing wildly in thought from past tense to present tense to the future and back again. I can't help but think it is a pendulum that has served me well, giving me balance and perspective. It is why the study of history is so very important. Balance helps you understand as Winston Churchill said what is vital and permanent, what is lasting and memorable. 2020 was one of those times we recognized history when it was happening. We tired of the overuse of words like "unprecedented" or "uncertain times" or that we needed to "pivot" during the pandemic. Fatigued or not we knew history when we saw it and we instinctively sought out our roots.

Through it all plants helped save the day.

I Need to Change My Plants

> ***When everything seems turned upside down, plants are reassuringly rooted. From the beginning of time; they are right side up. They are hopeful and a sign of life. They are healing. They set an example as they reliably follow the seasons, adapt to nature and weather the storms.***

When a storm occurs and a large tree is uprooted we take notice. It makes for good footage in news reports covering the calamity. We count on plants to be there, and, maybe in our hectic, digital technology-laden busy lives, we have taken them for granted to a degree. But in a time of turmoil they became less of a commodity and more of a way of life. And when things went upside-down each of us sought out our very own **"Vine and Fig."** Everyone has their eventual vine and fig and we certainly don't want to be afraid. This is one of those moments. What we do with it is up to us. Fear, anger, blame, if present, should be only short-term emotions and certainly are not part of the solution moving forward. What is your vine and fig? If you haven't identified it you need to change your plants then rest in its shade.

Rick Vuyst

And so the year is ended
the halls are decked so splendid
Oh tannenbaum in the corner
Fragrant natural foreigner
A friend that we've befriended

Chapter Twenty

Owl be Home for Christmas

LATE IN THE GROWING SEASON along the Lake Michigan shoreline, common milkweed *Asclepias syriaca* is distributing its seed. The seed pods jettison their flat brown seeds attached to tufts of silky fibers or floss. The pods split open along a central seam and then like parachutes are carried aloft by the wind. Milkweed is named for its characteristic milky sap or latex. Some prefer to call it silkweed due to the proliferation of the "seed floss" distributed when the pods crack open. It's an ingenious and natural propagation insurance for the distribution and continuation of the species, much to the merriment of the Monarch butterfly.

During World War II Dr. Boris Berkman, a Chicago physician and inventor had other ideas than a natural distribution. He wanted them harvested and used for the war effort. The milkweed, long considered by many a nuisance weed, in his mind would come to the rescue of aviators and sailors. For years, kapok would be used as the typical filler for floatation devices. The tree *Ceiba pentandra* produces a light and strong fiber known as kapok and it was used to fill mattresses, pillows and yes life preservers. Kapok was cultivated in the rainforests of Asia and Indonesia (Dutch East Indies). With the world at war, including the Pacific, the supply of this important filler was cut off. A replacement material was needed to spare the downed pilot or overboard sailor and Berkman had the solution. The common milkweed.

> *"What is a weed? A plant whose virtues have not been discovered."*
> *– Ralph Waldo Emerson*

Not only was milkweed plentiful in North America it could arguably do a better job than kapok as filler in life vests. Tests conducted by the U.S. Navy showed that a little over a pound of milkweed floss could keep a sailor floating in the water for hours.

The Gift that keeps giving

Money was appropriated by a congressional agriculture committee to build a processing facility. But someone would have to harvest the ripe milkweed pods. A laborious proposition, the general public would have to step up to contribute to the war effort at just the right time during the year. It was labor intensive work and an understanding of the plant would be needed. That's where the U.S. Office of Education stepped in to encourage children in schools to participate in pod collection. It was perfect timing as schools could organize the kids and educate them to pick pods while they were ripe but not yet fully open. Picking too early or too late would mean the opportunity that came along once a year would be missed and lives were hanging in the balance. Adults, school teachers and children rallied to the cause and once again civic pride and duty as well as plants had saved the day. The common milkweed had participated in botanical heroics like many other plants throughout the ages for medicine, shelter and in this case the rescue of those at sea. Year in and year out, season after season, plants have proven they truly are the gift that keeps giving.

The fruitcake of plants

The gift that keeps being given has got to be the Christmas cactus. Legend has it there are Schlumbergera, better known as Christmas or Holiday cactus, that become family heirlooms passed on from generation to generation. The gift that keeps giving. I know this to be true and it creates pressure for those receiving the inheritance. You don't want to be the one breaking the cycle of care for the beloved family species. In the wild, the species of *Schlumbergera* grow either on trees (epiphytic) or on rocks, making them very different from what you would normally consider a cactus. The stems are composed of segments. The segments are strongly flattened cladodes which means a flattened leaf-like stem with "wings." The modern genus *Schlumbergera* is credited to Charles Lemaire in the mid 1800s. It is named after Frédéric Schlumberger, who had a collection of cacti at his chateau near Rouen France.

> *"Now I am an old Christmas tree, the roots*
> *of which have died. They just come along,*
> *and while the little needles fall off me,*
> *replace them with medallions."*
>
> *– Orson Welles*

Oh the poor tannenbaum. Cut down at a young age only to be placed in a tree stand and situated in a stuffy warm corner and dressed in baubles. Left to tower over carefully wrapped packages with its bright lights and tinsel, it goes out in style soon to be relegated to the compost heap. No longer an evergreen.

Every year for over 40 years I have participated in the tradition of helping families pick out their Christmas tree. The outdoor temperature and precipitation dictate the speed at which they make the family corporate decision of which pine will join

I Need to Change My Plants

them for the holiday season. I spend the day lugging the specimens to tie them to the top of their vehicles and send them on their way. By the end of the day the redolent presence of all of me is the rich aroma of pine, fir and spruce. My jacket, shirt, pants, underwear, socks, shoes, hair contain evergreen needles. They find their way to the floor as I prepare to shower. I need to change my pants.

When I was young in the 1960s the solution to the needle conundrum was aluminum artificial trees. Space-age fashion, the birthplace of this new-age shimmering fad, was in Manitowoc, Wisconsin, which sits on the shore of Lake Michigan about 80 miles north of Milwaukee. A symbol of 1960s kitsch, the gaudy glamour was affordably available to all in silvery aluminum or pink, green or blue.

The Aluminum tree could be accessorized with a spinning color wheel set on the shag-carpeted floor and illuminated by a burning hot incandescent light bulb. The bulb would illuminate the spinning colors on the wheel plugged into a socket to rotate and magically change the tree's appearance. I inherited one just a few years ago and the receipt was still in the box. Purchased at an after Christmas sale the price paid was $1.25 plus tax. I plugged it in and, still functional, it became very hot, reminiscent of the old Easy Bake ovens kids would get as gifts at that time. I unplugged it before it started a fire and donated it to an antique collector who would revel in the nostalgic benevolence.

The aluminum tree and rotating wheel, when positioned close to the old television, sporting all of three channels and rabbit ears antennas, improved the TV's reception. That's a good thing as about that time we would all gather around and view, what starting in 1965 became a household tradition and national sensation, watching the CBS Christmas special *A Charlie Brown Christmas*.

> *"Let's face it. We all know that Christmas is a big commercial racket. It's run by a big eastern syndicate you know."*
> *– Lucy in a Charlie Brown Christmas*

Charlie, the director of the Christmas play is instructed by the real director, Lucy, to secure a pink aluminum Christmas tree for the pageant. Here is his chance to do something right for a change. At the tree lot, Charlie and Linus peruse the available trees as Linus raps with his knuckles on a pink metal tree that sounds like a hollow, lifeless, empty 55-gallon steel drum. Charlie Brown of course opts for the sad, small drooping real tree already dropping its needles.

> *"Gee do they still make wooden Christmas trees?"*
> *– Linus in a Charlie Brown Christmas*

Charlie and Linus bring the tree back, only to have Charlie become the subject of ridicule and laughter from the cast and recipient of the wrath of Lucy for his blockhead effort. "Rats" says Charlie Brown. In the spirit of the holidays and the evergreen symbol of hope, eventually the children of the Peanuts Gang rally around Charlie Brown and his sad, little tree.

Every year at the end of the Christmas tree selling season just prior to Christmas I go out looking for the last unwanted trees left on the lot to find them a good home. The remaining stragglers no one wanted, an outlier in need of encouragement and support. Though bent and needle cast, lonely and homely, the remaining trees are a symbol of vulnerability waiting for a sympathetic soul understanding of their plight. Finding them a home just in the nick of time gives me a warm feeling and nostalgic sentiment of days gone by and a time that was more simple. As a space-age boy I have a unique understanding of how the space race launched us into an age of satellite technology and aluminum trees and **how the sad lonely leftover evergreen can ground us once again.**

I remember tinsel in the tree hung haphazardly throughout. The tree would shed the strands throughout the Christmas season with a large share of it ending up in the vacuum cleaner. Much of it was persistent as made evident when the tree was removed from the house after the holidays and laid to rest by the curbside for pickup. As it lay forlorn for about a week until finally picked up, the remaining tinsel would hang on for dear life in January blizzard winds, a roadside monument to the post holiday blues. Meanwhile, back in the house, from time to time hidden in the shag carpet would be a random ornament hook to be stepped on while walking barefoot to the coffee pot on a February morning.

It was a time to unwrap Lincoln logs and erector sets on Christmas morning; Hot Wheel cars on orange-looped tracks; Bubble lights and C9 Christmas lights that would get hot and continually go out or break, especially when you would step on them or try to untangle them, and wearing out the batteries on your Operation game as you played it for the one hundredth time. Getting creative with your Etch-a-sketch tablet while Dean Martin sings Marshmallow World on the record player. Nibbling on Chex mix after a dinner that included green bean casserole. Food, like plants, brings people together. Cranberry sauce, hot apple cider and fruitcake. Mashed potatoes and pumpkin pie. Yams and salads.

Having worked in the retail sector my whole life, I suppose it explains childhood memories of holiday season shopping that are embedded in my mind. My Mom and Dad would take us kids to places like Sears, S.S. Kresge and Montgomery Ward to shop before the Christmas season. Wards was a magical place for a kid with the ride up the escalator to the second floor culminated by a large, decorated Christmas tree. In 1939, as part of a Christmas promotional campaign, Montgomery Ward staff copywriter, Robert L. May, created the character Rudolph the Red-Nosed Reindeer in a poem with the store distributing six million copies of the poem as a storybook. Later the song *Rudolph the Rednosed Reindeer* became a Christmas tradition thanks to the singing cowboy Gene Autry. Those were the days. It gave me a twinge of sadness and melancholy nostalgia when on December 28, 2000, at the turn of the century after lower-than-expected sales during the Christmas season, Montgomery Ward announced it would cease operating, close its remaining 250 retail outlets, and lay off its 37,000 employees. All stores closed within weeks of the announcement. Montgomery Ward was liquidated by the end of May 2001, ending a 129-year brick and mortar enterprise and for me a Christmas tradition.

A 1965 Christmas time visit to S.S. Kresge, founded by Sebastian S. Kresge, a traveling hardware salesman in the late 1800s, better known as KMart, is a childhood memory I won't forget. I was 6 years old at the time. The store was known for "Bluelight Specials," surprise deals that were announced in-store and offered for only 15 minutes, creating a dramatic rush for a bargain. I remember a cold, wet snow coming down on a Saturday evening, and my Dad on the hunt for a blue light bargain on a cut Christmas tree. My Dad was from Holland and had survived the Hunger winter of 1944-1945 during WWII. He was one for a bargain and knew how to find them. On the way to get the tree we first stopped for gas. My Dad, now 90 years old, says those were the good old days when gas was 17 cents a gallon; they would call you sir, pump it for you and give the three kids in the back seat a chocolate bar. An old car, I remember the fumes in the backseat. My Dad would always tell them to fill up the oil and check the gas. Then it was on to McDonalds where even today he remembers the hamburgers and french fries on the menu were only 15 cents.

We arrived at KMart and my Dad was successful in purchasing a sad bargain Scotch Pine cut Christmas tree for 75 cents.

I Need to Change My Plants

The green needles were sparse and the trunk was gnarled and very bent. I remember my Dad trying to set up the tree and mumbling it was more crooked than a career politician. Once loaded with ornaments, lights and tinsel to disguise its homely appearance, much to my Dad's chagrin, the tree fell over a number of times during the yuletide. My Dad needed to change his plants as in the family tannenbaum. He gave up on the first one midseason and bought a second 75-cent tree. This contorted sapling with serpentine trunk was worse than the first. He managed to wire it to maintain some semblance of posture and decorum until late December at which point it was out the door. Under the cover of darkness he stood it up in our neighbor's landscape where it remained unnoticed for a few months until it fell over. Our neighbor changed his plants by removing the transplanted tannenbaum and properly putting it out of its misery. At the time the merry malfunction of that tree added some stress to my Dad's holiday, but in the end it was foundational to a lot of family laughs and memories.

> **I need to change my plants:** When you change your attitude from "I'm tired" to "I'm seasoned" your experience will benefit others.

Is it hoot in here or what?

The Christmas tree of course has been the source of years of family memories and antics. Everyone has some sort of John Randolph moment as the resident Clark Sr. or "Dad" in the *Christmas Vacation* movie. Squirrel! When a squirrel gets in the house, or the tree for that matter, it's everyone for themselves. Fortunately squirrels seem content during the holidays with dodging bustling holiday traffic and raiding the birdfeeder. Squirrels are a polarizing topic, as I have some friends who shoot them and eat them, and I have other friends who intentionally feed them and make backyard "furniture" for them like miniature picnic tables. They have to stay busy. The squirrels that is. In winter their high-flying hijinxs to eat your sunflower seed can be fun to watch. I'm sure they enjoy it far better than splooting in summer. Squirrels sploot in the heat of summer when it's hot outside. They spread eagle on a cool surface like damp concrete sprawled out on their belly on a 95-degree day to cool down. You would too if you were dressed in fur; they're all dressed up with someplace to go. They seem to enjoy the chilly temperatures and holiday weather, so they're not so interested in getting inside anyhow. It was with great amusement during the Christmas season of 2019 when a Georgia family made the national news when they noticed one of the "ornaments" turning its head in the Christmas tree. Upon closer inspection they realized there was a screech owl which had taken residence on the interior of the tree and moved in with the festive family tannenbaum. Owl be home for Christmas. Is it "hoot" in here or what?

Captain Santa

I climb the forested back dune as the roar of the wind sails across the treetops above me. The muffled rumble of the waves can be heard in the distance as I make my way to the top. Once I crest the dune the wind hits me in the face with all its unobstructed force. I have the wind speed at about 20 knots on the foredune and down to the beach, the cold, late-December wind pelting me with gusts of airborne sand particles. Living along the Lake Michigan shoreline, it is a Christmas-eve tradition for me to walk to the shoreline regardless of the weather and look for the Rouse Simmons. Some call it the Christmas Tree Ship others call it the Ghost ship. Legend has it you can spot the ship or hear the ship's bells if in the right place at the right time, sometime between Christmas eve and dawn Christmas morning. I envision the old schooner fighting the wind and the waves with tattered sails foundering in the water. I face into the northwest wind looking towards Wisconsin but yet again this year to no avail. I turn to begin the ascent of the foredune with its frozen marram and sand reed grass glistening on the bank. The goal now simply to clear the crest to the protection of the backdune freed from the icy blast.

Built just after the Civil War in 1868 by Allen, McClelland & Co. in Milwaukee, Wisconsin, by 1912, the Rouse Simmons was one of the last vessels still sailing Lake Michigan in the golden age of sail. Grandiose schooners at the time with their wind swept sails they filled Great Lakes harbors. In 1912 sailing vessels such as the Christmas Tree Ship were nearly extinct, about to be sidelined by advances in technology. A three-mast schooner with a hull made of wood, 124.2 feet in length, 27.6 feet in breadth and 10.1 feet in depth of hold, the creaking wooden schooner must have been a sight to see, sailing low in the water loaded with Christmas trees in route to Chicago. The Rouse Simmons captain, Herman Schuenemann, inherited the moniker Captain Santa for his exploits navigating Lake Michigan's tempestuous attitude in November to pick up a load of Christmas trees from Northern Michigan and return them to the Clark Street bridge in Chicago. In the late 19th and early 20th centuries, the popular German tradition of decorating an evergreen tree in the home was now rooted in our culture and widely practiced. It made the entrepreneur's risky venture of a late-season voyage on the lake worth the gamble to deliver Christmas cheer. Herman would sell them, along with giving some to needy families. Schuenemann gave away many of his trees to the city's churches and poor. Over time his benevolence earned him both respect and the moniker Captain Santa.

The Rouse Simmons had sailed for the Great Lakes lumber trade for years. Lumber mills had circled the interior Muskegon lake where I live and was big business in the late 19th century. At the time transport via sailing ships was an efficient way to bring the resource to growing cities like Chicago. It was only natural that, despite the threat of tumultuous waves and weather, without the weather-predicting capabilities we have today, the danger of transporting Christmas trees in November was a natural offshoot for commerce.

By 1912 the Rouse Simmons was an archaic and tired vessel, but still functional depending on who you asked. Legend had it maybe Schuenemann didn't have the funds to do the necessary maintenance, but saw an opportunity, because winter weather had caused other ships to hesitate or cancel their voyage for trees. He saw it as an opportunity to make some extra profit and pay off his debts. He felt if the ship was loaded, including the top deck with thousands of trees it could be a payday for him. Instead the deck was stacked against him. Rats are wily and wary mariners and were deserting the ship, a sign to the sailors on board that the ship was ill fated and about to meet its destiny.

I imagine for Schunamen, purchasing an aged schooner would be profitable if he could wring the last bit of life from the tired vessel. You would also think that trees or lumber as exposed cargo would not be damaged or affected by weather and that they are somewhat buoyant compared to other commodities. Yet with the hull full on a leaky schooner and top deck loaded, the wet and ice covered trees added a lot of weight. With eight feet of trees piled exposed on the deck it is surmised it may have destabilized the craft. I have read accounts where those who witnessed its departure from Thompson, Michigan to head south, observed the vessel with less than a foot of freeboard above the water line due to the weight of the trees. A floating forest.

Before departure, Schuenemann invited a number of lumberjacks aboard to catch a ride back to Chicago to spend the holidays with friends and family. From all accounts it appears he was a kind-hearted soul who embraced his reputation as Captain Santa. With the Rouse Simmons, now fully loaded with evergreen Christmas trees, Captain Schuenemann knew the dangers of sailing in November, but the Christmas tree merchant had to get trees to Chicago. The clock was ticking and the Christmas season was on its way.

With barometric pressure dropping and the winds increasing, the winds and waves battered the ship as the Great Lakes often do in November. Two men checking the lashings on the trees as well as a small life boat were swept overboard along with a number of trees never to be seen again. The Rouse Simmons was spotted flying a distress flag, flying its flag at half-mast, a universal sign of distress five miles offshore while being driven southward by a northwest gale. Driven by the northwest winds I can only imagine what it was like on board. As one who lives on the Lake Michigan shoreline and has personally witnessed the lake acting more like an ocean than a lake, its power and a cold northwest wind is unforgiving and relentless, especially in November. A rescue boat was sent out to find them as they were reportedly spotted in the far distance riding dangerously low in the churning waters. A lifeboat was dispatched from Two Rivers, Wisconsin in the hopes of intercepting the south bound Simmons to bring the crew to safety. The lifeboat never found the vessel and crew. The Rouse Simmons had vanished, slipping below the surface deep into the cold waters of the big lake. The three-masted schooner went down on the afternoon of November 23, 1912 and laid to rest in roughly 165 feet depth of water. I have seen varying accounts of how many died that fateful day going down with the Rouse Simmons and its cargo of Christmas trees. It is not well documented exactly how many lost their lives, but estimates are eleven or twelve sailors, some lumberjacks along for the ride, co-owner, Captain Charles Nelson of Chicago, and one Herman Shueneman, Captain Santa. It is believed a ship will scream out after it is lost at sea.

Maybe it's the sound of air escaping from the hold of the ship when crushed by the pressure and weight of the depths, a tragic sound bemoaning the loss of human life.

Upwelling for decades stirred up the lake bottom, causing trees presumed from the Rouse Simmons ill-fated cargo as fragments of trees to appear in the water and on the shore. Even in the disaster Hermann Schueneman was delivering his trees. When winds blow across the lake's surface, pushing surface water away, water then rises up from beneath the surface to replace the water that was pushed away. This process is known as upwelling. We experience upwelling events along the lakeshore where I live from time to time in summer. One July day the water can be a swimmable 70 degrees and the next a frigid 40 or 50-something degrees after an upwelling event. When you feel the frigid water at a temperature very unlike the surface water you can imagine the evergreens would have retained their needles for a long period of time. And as noted in legend and song the Great Lakes never gives up her dead. Hermann's body was never recovered, but his wallet was netted by a fisherman in 1924 complete with newspaper clippings of his exploits as Captain Santa. It was well preserved even though it had been submerged for 12 years at that point.

It's considered good luck to nail a horseshoe to a vessel with the open end pointed up "to hold the good luck in." When the Rouse Simmons was eventually discovered by a diver in Lake Michigan in 1971, the horseshoe was hanging upside down by a single nail. The aging schooner's luck had run out.

Over the years, the schooner's disappearance spawned legends and tales that grew ever larger with the passage of time. Sailors believe a ship has a soul of its own. Through the years some Lake Michigan mariners have claimed to have spotted the Rouse Simmons appearing out of nowhere. Phantom ship bells are heard. Therein my imagination and annual Christmas eve jaunt over the dune. Through the years, looking to the northwest in the direction of Manitowoc and Two Creeks, Wisconsin on Christmas Eve or Christmas morning before dawn, I have never caught a glimpse of the ghost ship. It is said if lucky enough to have a moonlit night you can catch a glimpse of her with her sails ripped to tatters and wildly flapping about as if blown by gale-force winds.

Today for many the journey of the Rouse Simmons did not ***end*** below the surface of Lake Michigan but rather ***continues*** as a story and a legacy of how someone was trying to make an impact and found joy in the journey, even if ill fated at that. It's another example of why I say history and storytelling is so important. It leaves a mark. In our personal sojourn, the journey and adventure of others teaches us to daily embrace our wayfaring ways.

Many times the best part is the anticipation – the pilgrimage, the process of getting there. Together. The gift *is* the journey. When I was younger the process knew better than me that it's about the process. Now with seasoning I know better. There is joy in the journey. Something I wish I had been taught in my earlier years. Instead of viewing change as "inevitable" in a foreboding kind of way ... change is the dose of magic in our personal odyssey and simply enhances the important memories of "the good old days" as a foundation. Once you believe in magic ... each day becomes a gift. Even in the year 2020. So that's a wrap. Through it all we developed a 2020 vision. Take a "bough" and remember to change your plants.

"There is one elementary truth, the ignorance of which kills countless ideas and splendid plans: that the moment one definitely commits oneself, then Providence moves too. Whatever you can do, or dream you can, begin it. Boldness has genius, power, and magic in it.
  – Mountaineer William Hutchison Murray
  The Scottish Himalayan Expedition (1951)

About the Author

This is Rick Vuyst's third book. His first two titles were *I Just Wet My Plants* a book about his 25 years in broadcast radio and his garden show and *Operation Rumination* a book about selfless service and honoring veterans.

Rick Vuyst is host of the Flowerland show on NewsRadio WOOD 1300 and 106.9 FM and nationally on iHeart radio. Rick also was the "Mr Green Thumb" for WZZM TV 13 the West Michigan ABC television affiliate for over 20 years. He is part owner of Flowerland stores in Grand Rapids, Michigan where he has worked since 1976. In addition to gardening Rick is a health enthusiast, avid runner and loves photography on the Lake Michigan shoreline and in the garden where he lives in West Michigan. You can learn more by visiting thankyouverymulch.com.

Rick Vuyst